THE BOOK ON TOTAL SEXY HEALTH

The 8 Key Steps Designed By Nature

Udo Erasmus

ISBN: 978-1772771084

Second Edition

PUBLISHED BY: 10-10-10 PUBLISHING
MARKHAM, ON
CANADA

Dedication

I dedicate this book to:

- All of you on this precious, fragile blue marble in vast space
- Lives lit up from within
- Global harmony where everyone feels cared for
- All basic needs fulfilled
- You who embrace the vision, embody and manifest it
- Your total sexy health that awaits discovery

Table of Contents

Foreword

*T*HE BOOK ON TOTAL SEXY *Health* profoundly touched me, and I recommend that you take the time to read it slowly, word for word. An unseen reality is the foundation of the visible, audible, and felt realities you know and live in. In it is the peace, power, health and clarity, as well as the truth and sexy that all humans seek. It is part of your nature, and becomes accessible to you at will as soon as you've discovered your need to know, have learned how to focus your awareness on it, and are committedly practicing this focus.

Udo Erasmus does a masterful job of teasing out and describing that indescribable foundation of *healthy, powerful and sexy*. He brings it palpably to life for you, and he also knows how to speak from that all-encompassing state of being.

I'm impressed with the possibilities that Udo opens up, and I'm fascinated by the insights and the ease with which the world could function for the benefit of all. I believe this book should be mandatory reading as part of basic education. Reading *The Book On Total Sexy Health* will answer many questions you have secretly asked and longed to have answered, and will powerfully enhance the quality of your time on Earth. Understand and apply the knowledge in this book, and use it to address the root cause of all the big personal and global problems whose solutions have eluded mankind for millennia and perplexed the human race.

Buy it. Read it. Apply it. Share it. Let it light up your life. Let it provide the self-knowledge that puts you back in charge of your world.

—Raymond Aaron
  New York Times Bestselling Author

PREFACE:
A Qualifying Personal Journey

No Easy Beginnings

L IKE MOST OF YOU, I did not grow up in a family of masters, kings, geniuses, billionaires or politicians. Exactly the opposite, I was born on a 'confiscated' farm, during 'The War' in Europe, where my family lost everything twice. In 1945, before I was three years old, I was a refugee child fleeing, on a wagon drawn by a horse that could barely walk, led by an exhausted mother alone with six children under six. All we had was the clothes on our back and some silver spoons, family heirlooms that were wistful reminders of a safer and more peaceful past forever gone.

Fear, anxiety and terror were constant companions as we ran from the Communist war machine rolling up behind us, and into the oncoming artillery fire coming from Allied planes. Protection was non-existent. Nowhere was safe. These feelings stayed with me for the first three decades of my life, and still sometimes visit me now.

My father, originally German-speaking from Latvia, was captured in Normandy in 1944 and shipped to a Red Cross supervised prisoner of war camp in the United States. This left my mother to look after us on her own. When the axle on the horse-drawn wagon broke down, so did the last of my mother's strength. Leaving four children behind with a farmer she'd never met, she hoped to survive and save two of her children, one on each hand, by going on foot across the fields. This was safer than staying on roads whose ditches were filled with dead people and horses. Eventually, my aunt Ena, my mother's sister who spoke fluent Russian, went back behind now enemy lines and found us. The farmer had dropped us off at an orphanage in Berlin, and its caretakers put us on a train heading toward Switzerland. She took us off the train and reunited us with our mother in West Germany.

My father returned from the war soured on human beings and even more on big institutions: government, religion, drug companies, medicine and business. The war had also cured him of any loyalty to the German 'Fatherland.' As displaced persons, we took up space there, and Germans having lost the war were frustrated and humiliated, and resented refugees.

It took six years to get our exit papers from Germany, and when I was 10, my family emigrated from West Germany and landed in a small town named Oliver in British Columbia, Canada. A year later, my father bough 112 acres of 'bush' land about 15 miles west of the town of Smithers in Northern British Columbia and built a house there that was four inches wider at one end than the other. We cleared 40 acres of the land by hand and by horse. I spent two years living in that house and the 'stump ranch' that surrounded it.

We had no electricity, running water, radio or TV. "I just want to be left alone," was one of my dad's favorite comments. "The world stinks," was a second, and a third was, "If it doesn't rain in my bed, I'm happy."

My North American childhood was comparatively quiet. I was a shy, withdrawn, fearful and insecure kid who read a lot of books. They were both exciting and safe. I also spent time in nature, which felt friendlier than my family environment. But I never went far, because I startled easily and sudden noises triggered anxiety. I pictured being trampled by a moose, torn apart by a bear, or worse.

In this setting, I became obsessed in finding out what I could rely on. My experience was that people were not reliable, trustworthy or protective, and that I was on my own. It was a difficult childhood. Although I was sensitive and felt judged and criticized, I was not an unhappy kid. But I certainly wasn't exuberant, either.

I mostly did well in school, because words on the written page and academic pursuits were both interesting and non-threatening. I also experimented a lot, often testing the limits of social, physical, family and natural laws. I wanted to try everything out, to learn from experience. That was for me the best kind of learning, and I got my share of education in the school of hard knocks.

Early Motivation

When I was six years old, we lived in Germany in the upstairs farmworkers' quarters in a barn that housed nine horses on a farm on which my father worked as a laborer. I remember that adults were argumentative and short-tempered. They often took their frustration with each other out on us kids. Whenever there was tension, I would shake. As time went on, I learned to be the kid who could break tension with jokes and goofiness. It was my survival skill, and I became quite good at it, but it was never my mission.

One day, when I heard yet another tedious argument between adults about topics that seemed trivial to me as a 6-year-old, a thought occurred to me, "There must be a better way to live. There's got to be a way in which people can live together in harmony, and I'm going to find out how."

That thought became my lifetime mission. It drove my interests and my activities, and it also determined the topics I studied when I finished school and enrolled in university. To this day, it still drives what I read and think about, what I say, design, develop and do.

Higher Education

An avid reader, my interests were in both literature and science. In the end, science won out over poetry and stories, because it seemed more 'practical'. I wanted to know how things work, and science was more about truth, while literature was more about perspectives.

From my world of chaos, I enrolled in science because I wanted to know the principles by which the planet I live on works. 'Science' means 'knowledge'. In science, I studied physics, chemistry and mathematics, but soon got bored with how theoretical these disciplines became. I couldn't see their practical, down-to-earth applications. Not that there weren't any, but I was more focused on harmony between people.

After I tired of the 'pure' sciences, I enrolled in biological sciences, because I wanted to know how life and creatures work, a topic that never grows old for me. Molecules, cells, plants, the seasons and the weather, animals and people are super-fascinating. When I look out through my bay window into the garden of colorful flowers and the leaves moving in the breeze near the bay beside which I live, I'm in awe.

Along with my studies of biological sciences, which included anatomy, physiology, natural history, biochemistry and genetics, I also enrolled in psychology, because I wanted to know how thinking works. Then I enrolled in medicine because I wanted to know how health works.

Helping people get healthy seemed like a good way to spend my life. If a person were sick, all I'd have to do, so I reasoned, is turn them back in the direction of health, give them a push, and watch them get better. But to do that, I'd have to know what health is. That's what I hoped to find out by studying medicine.

Sadly, I only learned about disease in medicine, and the Dean told me that the medical profession doesn't know what health is. "We're working on it," he said. I felt deeply disappointed. When I was told in my first year of medicine that a doctor should always sound as though he knows what's going on even when he doesn't, my career in medicine came to an end. We called it 'lying' on the farm. That was not okay with me.

At the end of that year, I left medicine and returned to biological sciences, where I got to study normal cells, tissues and creatures. In medicine, the emphasis is on sick cells and sick or infected creatures. Back in biosciences, I spent two years in graduate studies. Specializing in biochemistry and genetics, and working with fruit flies, I did research on 'chemically induced crossing over' (whatever the heck that might be!) in males of that species. I loved genetics, because I got to look into the control room of cells. The genetic code had been 'broken'. The transcription of genetic DNA into RNA, and the translation of RNA into proteins were hot topics. It was exciting, and I was excited.

I slept on a camp cot under one of the counters (benches, we called them) in the lab so that I could be close to my first love. During that time, the 1960's, I began to become more aware of disturbing global social issues, and they troubled me. After accepting a full scholarship to do my Ph.D. in Genetics in Chicago with one of the pioneers of that discipline, I changed my mind, turned down the opportunity, and left university. I was hungry for something else as yet unclear to me, but not covered in any of the courses I had taken.

For a couple more years, I sat in on classes in the arts: English literature, social psychology, philosophy and religious studies, but what I was looking for was not there, either.

Self-Knowledge

At 17, I remember first feeling an intense ache in my chest. I didn't know what it was, and I couldn't shake it by any of the physical, mental or outside distractions that I pursued. The ache was always there. There was no physical problem associated with it. I was quite healthy.

By the time I turned 29, I still did not have an answer for my restless heart. I'd already done my time with drugs and alcohol in my journey of personal development. Some people told me to ignore the hole in my heart, but I couldn't. Others advised me not to dwell on it because it would make me crazy. That did not work. All of my social projects did nothing to ease the ache. People told me to get a good job, get married and have children, and I did all three, but they all failed to make the pain in my chest go away.

I realized that there was no external fix for the enigma of this internal ache, but I still did not know what to do about it. There weren't, or at least I had not met, people who talked with any authority about this ache. I was disheartened. At 30 years old, I even left the city because I hated it. In my opinion there, was no life in it. Somehow, I missed the fact that the people, animals and plants in my city were full of life.

Together with my newborn son and his mother, we moved from Vancouver into a cabin in the woods, at 9,100 feet elevation in the mountains of Colorado. It was an idyllic place with morning sunshine, countless pine trees, powerful afternoon thunderstorms, air fresh with ozone after these storms, and quiet days followed by silent nights.

It should have been heaven, but that's not what I experienced. Within a week of arriving, I realized that what I hated in the city was there with me in the mountains. "Oh, $@#%!" I thought, "It's me and my attitude that is the problem here", but I did not know how I developed my negative attitude and had no clue about how to begin to dismantle it and develop a better one. This was a key insight for my continuing progress.

One evening, I expressed for the first time in my life that I did not have it all together, and that something was missing. Tapping my chest lightly with my fist, I said to the person I was with, "I know there's a perfection within me. I know I'm not connected with it, and I need to find someone who can show me a step." The next morning, while going out in the landlord's pickup truck to get firewood for the cabin, I heard an announcement on the radio about an event and a teacher, and the words clicked with what I had on my mind. I immediately decided that I had to go there. It was about 200 miles away. At that meeting, a person much younger than I said, "The peace you search for in the world is within you, and I can reveal you that peace."

I was skeptical but decided to check it out. On the slim chance that he COULD show me that peace exists within me, I wouldn't want to miss it, and if he couldn't show me, I'd just keep looking. That is how, in 1972, I began a practice of self-knowledge whose goal is to bring my incessantly wandering awareness back inside, in touch with life.

Self-knowledge became the most basic, most practical and most life-changing part of my education. Getting to know first-hand, from my own experience, what I am, what I have, and what I'm capable of has opened my perception to a profound inner ocean of answers. That ocean exists within you also. It exists within every living human being.

Once I knew, it made complete sense. Life is the all-powerful presence and knowledge within me. It weighs nothing but runs everything. It makes and directs my entire genetic program, and my cells' and tissues' biochemical systems, flawlessly. I'm not even aware of most of what it does. It digests my food, draws nutrients into my body, transports them where they're needed, and builds them into my biochemical body architecture. It repairs and replaces parts worn out. It builds a brain to coordinate everything that goes on in and outside my body. It beats my heart when I'm sleeping. And, it makes it unnecessary for me to pay attention to any of the millions of details of the physical complexity that is my body.

My most useful investment in myself became making time for a committed practice of bringing my awareness into the feeling of life. As I got better at this practice of self-knowledge, my constant heartache began to dissolve. In retrospect,

I understand that this ache was my heart calling my awareness to come back home inside to life. In all of us, it's where our wholeness, peace and sexiness reside.

It's become clear to me that the key to harmony is internal and already exists in each human being. Eight billion people can live their life lit up from within, because the light of life that lights us up is already present within each of us. It's simply a matter of looking inward into that light rather than only outwardly away from it.

When I connect with and experience the light I am, I feel completely cared for. Truth is, life has perfectly cared for my body through all the dramas I've witnessed and traumas I've suffered. Every moment, 24/7/365, life has loved me without any conditions.

Once I feel life's care for me, I can live in harmony with other people. As soon as I feel cared for, the desire to acquire more stuff in order to feel better evaporates. Instead of being willing to hurt others to get more, I'm now free to help them meet their basic needs.

Feeling cared for by life, I derive joy from caring for others. No sacrifice is necessary. I don't have to forego having all of my basic needs met. There is more than enough for all. Humanity suffers not from lack of resources, but from loss of heart. When we find our heart, we can solve all of the problems in the world with relative ease, because all of them began with heartlessness.

Always, my first step is to become more present and aware of my own being. I find the light in my personal world by mastering presence in my own life. Living life lit up from within is the noblest mastery and accomplishment for human beings.

Finding My Life's Work

In 1980, when pesticides poisoned me and the doctor had no remedy, I realized that my health is MY responsibility. I also knew that the bodies of most animals and all humans in nature are made from food, water, oxygen and sunlight, and nothing else.

I figured out that my first intervention when something goes wrong with health should be to raise the standard of quality of my intake of food, water and air, and to give my skin exposure to the sun. Searching through the journals for information on nutrition and health as well as nutrition and disease, and talking to people who knew more than I on that topic, I learned that every year, 98% of the atoms in my body are removed and replaced. I didn't know it at the time, but my body, like everyone else's, was a perpetual work in progress, a major construction site. That's what made it possible for me to heal physically from my poisoning.

It worked out beautifully in practice. To heal, I only needed to raise the quality of my intake of oxygen, water and food, and within one year, life re-built 98% of my body to a higher standard. There was my hope. I did that, and physical healing took place. There was my proof.

I found out how much industry damages oils when it treats these most delicate of our food molecules with harsh chemicals and then heats them to frying temperatures to extend their normally short shelf life. This learning revised my understanding of how oils should be treated in order to optimize health rather than to destroy it. I concluded: Oils should be made with health in mind. We should protect them from being damaged by light, oxygen and heat.

Out of that simple idea, a new industry of making oils with health in mind was born. In 1986, flax seed oil came out of my invention of the new method for making oils, and several companies now make it. Directly or indirectly, they all learned from me how to do it.

After I had moved back in with my mother in order to write my book on oils (*Fats and Oils*, which I later expanded and renamed *Fats That Heal Fats That Kill*), she asked me to move her dahlia bulbs. A life-long avid gardener, she was getting older, and her energy was becoming less than her ambitions.

xxii   The Book on Total Sexy Health

I said to her, "You know, mom, I don't see moving your dahlia bulbs as the purpose of my life." I thought she'd be angry, but she matter-of-factly said, "Oh! What DO you see as the purpose of your life?" We were both floored, jaws dropping, by what came out of my mouth. Here's what I answered:

"I will make sense of how fats and oils affect health."

"I will create a comprehensive, practical, consumer-friendly field of health."

"I'll create a comprehensive, practical, consumer-friendly field of human nature."

She was floored because her problem child had finally come up with a purpose. I was floored by how clear I was about what that purpose was. I'd thought about what to do with my life for years, but had never clearly formulated a life's work and mission. "Okay," she said. "I'll get someone else to help me with my dahlia bulbs."

My first purpose, regarding oils and health, has been accomplished. The two others, health and human nature are so intertwined that I've linked them together. Under the umbrella of total sexy health, I can address every problem on the planet. Why? Everything affects health, and there is now great interest in this topic, and even more interest in being sexy, which depends on health. Health was invented by life in nature and is based in nature and human nature. It is a huge, important and practical topic.

Trauma Can Be A Great Gift

'Sexy' is the word most people use to denote presence, vitality and appeal. What most people don't realize is that health is the foundation of 'sexy.' TOTAL SEXY HEALTH is a system that, once you understand and apply it, you can effectively address all of the problems on the planet, beginning with your own. You can identify in which part of human nature each problem began, and then intervene to fix it at that level. Ultimately, you can help others live more abundant lives, assist them to become more fully present in all of their being, and provide insights toward their personal mastery of life and living.

With all its pain, my difficult childhood generated many insights and discoveries, which have the potential to turn the world around into the kind of peace-filled, kind and harmonious place it could and I want it to be.

In my view, every human being is on life's team. The master is life inside each one of us. Some people are highly functional on life's team and its mission of living lit up from within, in harmony and with everyone's basic needs fully met. Some people are not yet clear, but they're still on the team. Still others interfere with the mission, because they do not yet know this magnificent possibility.

We now know that anything anyone does anywhere on this planet affects everyone everywhere. In the time I have, I will inspire, inform, empower and entertain as many members of my team as possible. Wish me luck, and work with me. Better still, deepen your connection, take your instructions, and work with the master: *life within you.*

INTRODUCTION:
What is Total Sexy Health?

Total

WHAT IS TOTAL? TOTAL IS all-inclusive. Total is global. Total involves all aspects. Here, total means 'fully present in the eight parts of your being and your contexts'. Total includes all aspects of nature and human nature that affect feeling sexy and being healthy. If it sounds mysterious, don't worry. I'll walk you through it. As you read this book, the mystery will be hacked and unpacked, you'll get more clarity on what each one of the eight parts is, and you'll know what you can do to get each of them under your belt.

Total means everything is there, with nothing left out. In popular press and common understanding, health involves food and fitness, but the truth is that while fitness and food are part of it, they're only a small part of total health. Total includes what you can learn from using all of your senses and being to observe life, both within yourself and around you.

Total includes all of your nature: presence, life energy, inspired creativity, physical body and survival smarts. It also includes the bigger picture: your social, natural, planetary and 'extraterrestrial' (solar system, galaxy, cosmos) contexts. Total is the full, entire amount of something, and includes all your positive and negative feelings, all your thoughts and imaginings, and all your inner impulses and outer reactions.

Total means 100% and contains all opposites. Total includes life and death, pain and pleasure, and sickness and wellbeing. It embraces darkness and light, love and hate, and inside and outside. It spans silence and sound, nothing and everything, and emptiness and fulfillment. It encloses both depression and inspiration.

Total includes consciousness and energy; perception, interpretation and memory; thought, word, action and outcome. It's the whole that includes what we ignore, what we learn and what we know.

Total means complete, and includes many levels. There's space, time, energy and matter, and the energies of light, sound, feeling, smell and taste. Total material levels include electrons, protons, atoms, molecules, and macromolecules. Body levels include organelles, cells, tissues, glands and systems. Social system levels include individuals, families, communities and nations. Planet levels include sunlight, air, water, land and ecosystems. Levels beyond these include solar systems and galaxies. All of these affect health, and all do so in different ways.

Total includes being alone and being with others. By total health, I mean: addressing all of it. It involves both being and doing. It involves attention to all inner and outer events in life. It includes the heavenly bodies, the space within which they unfold, and the forces that create, maintain and move both.

Total sexy health includes all that creates, maintains, damages and repairs. Since the truth is that EVERYTHING affects health, we must give EVERYTHING its due. Total sexy health literally embraces all of everything.

Since everything affects health, everything affects sexy. To be totally sexy, you have to be totally healthy. To be totally healthy, you have to give each of the eight parts of total health the care and attention it needs. This might seem like a tall order, but it becomes easier once you know the simple basics that I'm beginning to share.

What's made it difficult to get optimum sexy is that you don't know what exactly makes you sexy. Until now, you've had no road map. In this book, you'll get an overview of the missing road map. Doctors and drug companies' ads tell you to take more responsibility for your health. But disease management systems do not dispense knowledge of health care, and those who tell you to take a more active role in your health do not provide you with practical ways to do so. How will you give health its due without guidance? It's not possible. Here, you'll get helpful guidance toward total sexy health.

Sexy

Almost everyone wants to be sexy, but hardly anyone knows what makes you sexy, and how to deliberately go about being, becoming, remaining or reclaiming sexy. When you don't know, you easily fall victim to fakery that promises to make you sexier but doesn't deliver. You remain a sucker of everybody's pitch on sexy until you know the truth about the nature of sexy.

Knowing what's sexy gives you your power back. When you know how to show up sexy, you own your world. It'll eat out of your hand. Living will be good fun and will enhance the happiness you can know. Do you want to have more fun and be happier by being sexier? Most people do. It's okay if you don't. It's your right to remain out of touch with your deepest innate beauty. What is within you is in its nature already sexy. It wants to come out of the closet into which you've been forced to stuff it, to express itself gloriously. The deepest drive of every living human being includes being personally powerful by being radiant, vibrant and attractive.

What is sexy? It depends on whom you ask. Ask a friend. One of my friends said, "Sexy is an attitude. If you think you're sexy, you are sexy." "Is that all there is to it?" I asked him. "Yup!" he answered. "What if you can't convince yourself?" I then asked. "Then you're not sexy," was his reply.

For him, sexy is something you talk yourself into, but he

confessed that he had never thought much about it. Most people, including me until recently, have not tried to nail down what sexy is made of in life. When I began to think about it, I realized that I know a lot about what is sexy. We all do. You'll see as you read this book that you know much more about sexy than you've ever acknowledged. And you'll find that you have more control over what it takes to be sexy or even sexier than you've ever believed you had.

Most people define sexy by a way of thinking, based on limited experience and even less deep thought. Defining sexy that way limits sexiness because thoughts are by their nature limiting and limit-producing.

Look up 'sexy' in the dictionary. Understandably, many of its meanings are related to lust, arousal and seduction. They include steamy, lewd, risqué and x-rated. But another set of meanings of 'sexy' embraces a far wider, more positive and less sex-related words that include tantalizing, provocative and stimulating, as well as exciting, alluring and passionate.

In common usage, 'sexy' describes many topics that have nothing whatsoever to do with sex. The word 'sexy' is often used to denote something that's creative and edgy, but also protective, social and natural. We talk about sexy technology, sexy ideas, sexy poems and melodies and sexy lines in art. People call sexy whatever attracts their attention and makes them take notice. Anything vibrant, lit up or lively, fun and engaging is 'sexy.' In fact, in street talk, 'sexy' includes what in the past was called whole or holy, and sacred, inspired or energized. Even what's spirited and spiritual is called 'sexy'.

True 'sexy' is not based on the fads, images or thoughts that human beings invented. Sexy is inherent in nature and human nature. Natural 'sexy' is powerful and much broader than you think. It is what you already are in your nature beyond your fantasies. In fact, your fantasies often detract from your true 'sexy'. Beyond them, you can bring your awareness to 'sexy' to let it shine out.

Sexy, like health, is your natural state. Sexy is not just about having sex, the delicious activity that takes up a small part of most days–like 2 minutes on average and a few hours if you struck erotic gold–but also about being, feeling, looking and sounding lit up from within.

You exude sexy when you feel fulfilled, radiant or magnificent. Confident and in awe of life, you emit sexy. All of these are possible for you at will, all day, every day if you want. Is it that simple, and is it really possible? Absolutely! How? Read on.

I'll post a longer and still growing list of words that people use to describe what makes you look, sound, feel and enjoy 'sexy' on the website: www.totalsexyhealth.com. Send me your favorite words for 'sexy'. I'll add them to the list for everybody to enjoy.

Sexy is not arrogant, pushy or flaunting, nor self-effacing, pretentious or boastful. Sexy is not mean or overbearing. Sexy is not chronically angry, sad or fearful. Sexy is not full of complaints.

Sexy covers a lot of territory. Some aspects of sexy are subtle, while others are more obvious. The many aspects of sexy correspond to the different parts of nature and your nature. If you're alive, all parts of sexy already exist in you, and you'll become more aware of them as you learn and practice to access them.

There's a lot in the details behind the simple sentence that you've just read. Here it is again, said in another way. **Sexy predictably results when you live deliberately alert and present to existence in line with nature and your nature**. When you live aligned with the nature of any part of health, that part confers upon you its contribution to sexy. When you live out of line with it, that part of your sexy leaves the building. When you re-align with that part, you get its contribution to your sexy back.

'Sexy' sells everything. Savvy advertisers fool you into buying a wide range of products that promise to make you sexier, but sexy can't be brushed, painted or sprayed on. Contrary to what you've been promised, you can't roll, slather or lather it onto your body. You can't wear something to make you sexy. The truth is that YOU make clothing look sexy, not the other way around.

Using sexy as bait, some advertisers fool you into harming yourself at your own expense. A recent, huge study showed that soft drinks can almost double your risk of pancreatic cancer. Instead of hurting yourself with advertisers' false doctrines, nourish yourself with a return to the sexiness that nature built into you. Until you know what sexy actually is, you'll forever fall victim to commercial fads. Sex and sexy are key triggers in ads that get you to buy stuff that's cheap to make, expensive to buy, and profitable for someone else. In this book, I'm using sexy to sell you on yourself.

Health is the foundation of sexy. Since total health is made up of eight different parts of nature and human nature, total sexy is also made up of these eight parts. Sexy goes down as you drift and stray from one or more of these parts of nature and your nature. It returns as you come back into alignment with each part. You can reinstall each part of sexy in a systematic way. That's what you'll learn in this book and the interactive support materials on the book website: www.totalsexyhealth.com.

The system I developed for you makes it easy. Without a step-by-step system to follow, your odds of success are small. The steps to total sexy health are not MY steps. They are THE 8 key steps that nature designed.

Today, I heard someone say on the news that 'sexy' is a state of mind. But 'sexy' goes much deeper than mind and thought. 'Sexy' is a state of being. 'Sexy' is something you embody in all of your nature. As you become more aware of it, you embody and express 'sexy' in what you feel, think, say and do. Beyond words and emotions, 'sexy' is already your deepest state of being and your original nature. You reclaim your inborn sexy when you rediscover and come to know your essence, your life energy and your power.

Your heart, your core and your being are your source of 'sexy'.

'Sexy' is what, deep down, you are. You don't only do 'sexy.' You are, by nature, inherently 'sexy.' Sexy is not something you have to create. Sexy is a matter of self-responsible self-discovery. Discover it. I'll help.

Health

Total health is the foundation of totally sexy. Most of you desire and deserve to look, feel and be sexy. Most of you don't yet know the extent to which health is identical with sexy. Many people take care of some aspects of health but ignore other, equally important, aspects. If total health makes you totally sexy, do you want to know what total health is and how it works?

What is health? Health is your natural state. Health is the foundation of sexy. Health is vitality. Health is wholeness. Health is inner calmness. Health is a life lived from your infinitely calm foundation. The World Health Organization defined health as "total physical, mental and social wellbeing, not merely the absence of disease and infirmity." That's a start, but a lot more goes into total health than that.

Health is total presence in all of your being. Total presence includes inner peace, a life lit up, inspired creativity, a body fit and fed in line with nature, and survival smarts: handling stress and crisis with confident competence. Total presence in all of your being enables you to live an enjoyable life with reliable systems for protection and safety built in. Total presence includes social ease with others in mutual acceptance and cooperation, respecting nature, living in calm presence and accepting the timeless infinite.

The wholeness that's total presence in all of your being has eight parts, which are the eight key steps designed by nature to make you wholly sexy. Here's a preview of what's to come in the rest of the book on total sexy health.

1. **Health is awareness of inner contentment deep in the core of your being**. When you're aware down

into the depths of the rich feeling of your inner self, you know real, healthy, sexy peace. This is possible under any circumstance. The power of dwelling in the inner silence of your being, fully present, feels sexy and is attractive. This is true regardless of whether you're a young or old man or woman. Presence or inner awareness is the topic of Chapter One.

2. **Health is vital energy**. Vital energy is sexy. When you live lit up by life, you radiate. The radiation of light that results from being the life you are is highly attractive and gorgeously sexy. It is so sexy that it transforms plain, even scarred looks into spectacular beauty. Even when you're old and your face is deeply wrinkled, you become phenomenally beautiful the moment your eyes light up. The truth is that the energy of life is the essence of sexy. Life energy is the topic of Chapter Two.

3. **Health is the inspired creativity that life exudes**. Inspiration is the bridge between life and the physical world. Inspiration 'sexifies' you. From inspiration, you create. A feeling inspires creativity, from which you invent new images, words, thoughts, actions and results. Creating what has never been is sexy.

   Do you find poets, artists, dancers and musicians attractive? Inspired creativity makes them sexy. That's also true for writers, inventors and designers of gadgets that ease your pain or enhance the quality of your life. Be like that. Inspired creativity makes the world shine. Making the world shine makes you profoundly sexy. Inspired creativity is the topic of Chapter Three.

4. **Health is a body in line with nature**. You like fit bodies and good hygiene. You want fresh air, water and food. You celebrate efficient effectiveness and

excellent performance. Millions pay money to watch, with rapt attention, a highly specialized, entertaining physical performance with zero relevance to your survival. You call it 'sport'. It's sexy.

You admire skill. You adore grace and flair. You watch trained and disciplined human bodies with both awe and wonder. Track stars, dancers and gymnasts get your attention. So do skaters and snowboarders. Michael Jordan and Cirque du Soleil take the cake. Your sexy body is the topic of Chapter 4.

5. **Health is survival smarts: Competent response to stress, changes, crises and emergencies**. A confident voice in such situations is attractive. Decisive action to fight or avert danger is sexy. Leadership that protects others from harm is highly sexy. Calmness under fire is sexy. Courageous, bold protective acts and care are super-sexy.

    A Superman who can pierce steel with his eyes is far less of a hero and is less sexy than you standing fully present in danger and protecting and caring for the lives you live to serve. Courage is sexy. Survival smarts is the topic of Chapter Five.

6. **Health is social ease, grace and acceptance. It's also connection, reliability and contribution**. When you're comfortable within yourself in the company of friends, strangers or enemies, you're sexy. Keeping promises is sexy. When what you say and do line up, it's sexy. When you feel empowered in your own being, and use your power to empower others, you're incredibly sexy. When you lend a hand to help where help is needed, you are an example of check-me-out sexy. When you give others space to learn from their efforts and mistakes, then too you're sexy.

Sexy is about serving the totality of the human life cycle, from before conception until after the end of the body. Standing firm and tall in your truth in the face of powerful odds is sexy. Social connection is the topic of Chapter Six.

7. **Health is respect, reverence, and gratitude for nature.** Nature is sexy. Nature and your nature come from the same one source. You're a cell in the body of nature. Each cell has both autonomy and community. Each is independent, minds its own business, does what it has talent for, accepts what it needs from other cells and gives what it has extra. It does not hoard, and takes its instructions both from life and from the needs around it.

    You're conceived in nature, and you live and die in her. You're never separate from her, other than in a deluded mind. Your body is nature and belongs to nature. When you live and act in line with knowing that, you're naturally sexy.

    Nature is your environment, and provides all of your resources. Living sustainably and taking care of nature as nature takes care of you, is really sexy. Environmental health is the topic of Chapter Seven.

8. **Health is calm presence.** Calm presence is the acceptance of your temporary part in the infinite order of the universe. The phrase, "Relax. Nothing is under control!" nails it. You kill sexy by fighting what is. Conscious, calm and relaxed acceptance of what is, not by your small will, but by the will of the formless, nameless infinite power that creates everything. You're sexy when infinity flows through you and you know and feel it. Infinite awareness is the topic of Chapter Eight.

In summary, here are the 8 key parts of total sexy health designed by nature.

1. Presence/Internal Awareness
2. Life Energy
3. Inspired Creativity
4. Physical Body
5. Survival Smarts
6. Social Group
7. Natural Environment
8. Infinite Awareness

Principles And Components

Health is based on principles, which describe with precision the nature of things. Your acceptance of them makes your life easier because you're not fighting what is. When you fight what is, you become a victim of self-created departure from reality. Health results from your alignment with principles and components that you can use to create the degree of sexiness you want. Once you know and apply them in your life, you can control the mystery of sexiness by taking control of health.

Health is based on alignment with your essence, life and nature. As much as possible, make your own unique and personal connection, based on direct, personal experience of essence, life and nature. Seek experience. Search for what is true to life. Question what is widely believed, culturally popular and institutionally promoted. Examine what is historically mandated, educationally recommended, and legally imposed or enforced. Much of what you hear and read (and mindlessly repeat) is hype with weak foundation. Some of your fear-based, long-outdated superstitions need revision. Replace them with discoveries more closely aligned with life, nature and truth.

You can deliberately create sexy, no matter what your past,

your genetics, your history or your story is. If you're alive, you have all that you need to be sexy right now, right here, built in. If you don't feel sexy, where are you off? What are you missing? What don't you know? What's in the way? What are you not yet doing?

Distinct And Different

Why do you need to look at each of the eight key parts designed by nature that we just spoke about? The reason is simple. Each part of total sexy health is distinct and different. Each plays a unique role in total sexy health. For total sexy health, you have to give each one its due. Let me expand on that. Most people think of health as food and fitness. But total sexy health is much more than just physical. Food, fitness, recovery, digestion and detoxification are the pieces of the physical part of health. All together, they only make up only 1/8th of total sexy health.

My goal in this book is to outline all 8 parts. Mastering them all, you'll look better, feel better and accomplish more. You'll enjoy life more, think more productively and act more effectively for more consistent results. Living in alignment with nature and human nature brings you optimum enjoyment.

Let me repeat something I've already said. *EVERYTHING affects health, and everything affects sexy.* When you align with all eight different parts of nature and human nature, you get total sexy health. Each part provides one piece of the whole picture.

When you live the ultimate life of total sexy health, you achieve three goals. They sound complicated only as long as you don't know how simple they are to achieve. Once you know how, it's easy. Here are the goals:

1. You live your life lit up from within, fully present in all of your being, feeling whole and perfectly cared for

2. You live harmoniously with all of the other creatures with whom you share this planet

3. You ensure that the basic needs of all creatures are optimally met in a long term sustainable way

Each of the eight key parts of total sexy health makes a contribution to sexy. Each has a different nature and a different function. Each part needs a different kind of attention on a regular basis. Each part goes off in a different way, subtracting sexy from you, and each part responds to a different kind of intervention that brings its part of sexy back to you.

Most people believe that it's impossible in practice to attain a life lit up and in harmony, with all basic needs of all fulfilled. The truth is that all three are already part of your nature. You can attain them all, by doing the necessary personal, internal sexy-making homework within yourself.

Once you become aware of this fact and make the necessary effort, you discover for yourself that you are first and foremost the source of light, harmony and care in your life. When that becomes real as an experience for you, you become a model and source of the same possibility for others in your sphere of influence. In that way, light, harmony and care for the basic needs of all can expand to embrace everyone else living on this planet.

Who's Responsible?

Who's responsible for your total, your sexy and your health? Who benefits from mastery of total sexy health? The predictable answer to these simple questions is that sexy and unsexy in your life result from your presence or your lack of presence. They show your degree of attention or inattention. They result from your actions or inactions. They reflect your social comfort or unease. They come from your natural or your unnatural affiliations.

On the day that my doctor told me that she had no cure for

my pesticide poisoning, I realized that total sexy health is my personal responsibility. Self-responsibility is powerfully sexy. At 38, I already had the beginnings of arthritis. When I put even a bit pressure on my knees by slightly bending them, I felt pain. Now, several decades later, I have no pain in my knees or other joints, except for brief time spans after I bang into something. How did I become pain-free? I did what you'll read in these pages. I created this book so that you can apply it in your life, and have the same amazing, rich, love-filled life that I get to enjoy every day. What is in me is also in you, because both you and I are human. The key? Dig into the truths of all levels of being and align your life with these truths. **That is sexy.**

Become passionately interested in your foundation, your journey and your enjoyment of total sexy health. Start now. Be clear that neither you nor I created what I'm sharing with you. Life and nature created it. I want to know, so I ask, pay attention, discover and learn. I get to be a messenger who brings you what I've learned, to the extent that I've learned it. I'm still discovering more each day. Life and nature are as alive in you as they are in me.

Be aware of *life energy*, the perfect master that dwells within you. It runs the show you are, without demanding anything in return. It's the fullest and sexiest experience that exists. Discover and become that internal master. It provides you with rich experience, practical insight, deep motivation and clear direction. Awareness is the most expert source of knowledge on total sexy health.

Seek and be with people who acknowledge your equality and encourage and empower you to find and live your highest, healthiest, sexiest self.

Inner And Outer Territories Of Sexy

In your consideration of the eight parts of total sexy health, you'll come across material to which you had not given much thought. Most people only rarely observe, embrace or understand the inner territories of sexy. These, the areas of self-knowledge, include awareness, life energy, and inspired creativity. We'll emphasize these in this book, as they're now the areas that hold the greatest potential for improving the quality of life of human beings everywhere. Their neglect forms the greatest barrier to building a world that works for all, and poses the most serious threat to human survival.

However, even the least familiar material will have a ring of truth to it, because the eight parts already exist in your nature and surroundings. You've been dealing with them all your life. You're already competent in some of them. Less aware of others, you'll have 'aha' moments and insights when you recognize their nature and intrinsic value to you.

You'll not find me talking about something that's not part of you or the world in which you live. All of what you'll read here is common ground. It's not based in the differences between races, genders, cultures, religions and other man-made systems. It isn't based on ideas, beliefs, symbols or images. It's based on experiential knowledge of the existential and biological roots of what you and I are. For living, breathing, thinking, acting human beings, reliable results follow when you discover and align with nature and your nature. **Knowledge is sexy.**

You're much sexier than you've ever been told you are, and you may not have ever believed the extent of your potential. Here it is laid out for you, so you can choose to maximize the richness of your time on Earth (which is sexy), or you can decide that you want to live up to less than your full potential. The choice ever remains yours. **Choosing is sexy.**

By the end of the book, you'll have knowledge on which to base choices. Without knowing what is true, choices are just hopeful guesses. Guesses come with doubts, and doubts aren't sexy. Above, I've briefly laid out the territory we'll cover. So, let us begin together to fill in the details.

1

BEYOND HEALTH 1:
Presence, Internal Awareness

Invisible

PRESENCE, ALSO KNOWN AS INTERNAL awareness, is the first key part of total sexy health designed by nature. The wholeness, love, peace and fulfillment you want are always present in the space your body occupies. Internal awareness is being present to being present in that space. You can practice that. If you're not familiar with this, it sounds a bit abstract, but in truth, it is super-practical and important.

You might ask me, "Why do you begin this journey into health with something that no one can see or hear, and that can't be measured except by your own awareness? How will that help get and keep me well?" It's a good question that reasonable people ask.

My answer is this: The bush in your garden has roots that are invisible to you. These invisible roots are the source of the existence of the bush. You would be right to say that they are the power and essence of the bush. Destroy the bush, and a new one may grow from the roots. Destroy the roots, and the bush is finished. Just as the roots feed the bush, what is invisible in you feeds your more visible and obvious aspects. The invisible in you is vitally important. To live life fully, you need to know your invisible roots as well as your visible parts. Get to know your roots.

Let me say it another way. Every issue that you deal with is a symptom. Your problems in health, home, family, work, nation and nature are symptoms that you can notice, but their causes are deeper, mostly hidden from your view. Largely unknown to you, they remain unsolved. You can't fix a problem whose root cause escapes you.

What is BEYOND HEALTH? Beyond health is the invisible in you that can't get sick, degenerate, or die. Beyond health is that in you beyond your human life and your physical death. Death may not be sexy, but beyond death is sexy beyond sexy. It's really, really sexy.

Beyond health you find peace. In peace, which is beyond health, there's no darkness or light, no silence or sound, no emptiness or feeling, no pain or pleasure. There IS awareness. In peace beyond health, there is no time, space, matter or energy. In pure awareness, there's no circumference, form or movement, and no inside or outside. Beyond health is beyond thoughts and images. It exists as a reality that can't be grasped by your mind, but that can be known by relaxing and letting go of all limits and dimensions in your mind. The bliss of this 'knowing' is supremely sexy. It is your ultimate connection.

It hurts when you disconnect from the essential core of your being and the peace within it. The **pain** of disconnection, which you might feel as empty, blue, or restless, is your core calling your awareness to come back home to it. In you, that core is present everywhere (omnipresent), all knowing (omniscient) and all-powerful (omnipotent). Internal awareness is your infinite source, the dimensionless, endless, unified field. It is love without condition, and your ultimate home.

Beyond time, space, energy and matter, and also beyond thoughts, memories and imagination is the reality of ultimate being. Its power is real, but words cannot describe it. It is speechlessly sexy.

Solitude is the way to discover it. You can choose voluntary solitude in a safe place. There, you can find and discover the stillness of the invisible reality of being. It exists in the center of your being, and expands outward to the expanse of infinity. People who embrace the power of solitude are sexy. **Voluntary solitude is sexy.**

Pure, content-free awareness is the nature of the core of your being. It is a doorway to the fathomless universe that enfolds you. When you want to know it and are willing to sit perfectly still, you'll find that the door is open and the answers to your deepest longings are there for you.

You live in a world of symptom management, in which even the symptom management experts don't know the causes of the symptoms they suppress. Not knowing the root causes, they can't fix your problems. This is why illnesses and wars persist, and cures for them remain unavailable. In truth, something within you is the source of all your problems. Just slightly deeper, you can find all your solutions.

Lack of awareness of your internal foundation begins your problems. Awareness of that internal foundation makes practical solutions to your problems available and accessible. Aware and focused in stillness, you find sexy insights and knowledge. Stillness is the only known reliable practice for deepening insights. They are your best source of power, wisdom and manifestation. Live your life focused. Be focused in the present, which contains all that exists. Nothing is sexier than the present moment.

Becoming aware of being aware, you discover both the calm stillness that is awareness' nature, and everything else that unfolds in that stillness. Real, true, personal peace has its roots in the core of your existence beyond your senses. **Real, personal**

peace is sexy. With that awareness, you can solve the challenges and conflicts within you and surrounding you.

Look at the world. Peace has always eluded us, and we think that peace is impossible. The best we've gotten is temporary absence of war, which is not peace. Absence of war is more appropriately called a cease-fire.

We apply the same inverted logic of ignorance to many other topics. We don't know the nature of health, so we put up with mere management of disease. We don't know the nature of prosperity, so we create lifestyles based on debt. In each case, we 'peer into darkness to discover the nature of light'. Like ignorant fools, we try to find presence in absence.

When we do arithmetic, we know better. What is 2 + 2? We know that the right answer is 4. All other answers are wrong. Truth is, there are infinite-minus-one wrong answers. By knowing the one right answer, we automatically know all of the wrong ones, too.

What if you looked into light to get to know the nature of light? What if you examined the nature of peace to get to know it, beginning with yourself? What if you observed and felt your way into health? What if you stored value rather than perpetually accumulating and endlessly paying off deficits?

War, disease and debt have spawned institutions that have great power but fail to make their individual members' quality of life as rich, fulfilling and magnificent as it can be.

Within your being is something you've searched for all your life, but you've searched for it where you cannot find it. What you search for is not in the world outside you or in your mind and thoughts. Some people have tried to hijack and harness your search, to fulfill their own misguided agendas. The truth is that what you seek is and has always been right where you are. When you bring your awareness into contact with it and discover its nature, your life becomes fuller, richer and more enjoyable. And you find infinite possibilities and choices that enable you to build the life of your dreams.

As you get to know your mostly neglected foundation, an extraordinary life becomes possible and begins to unfold. In that personal foundation, all stress ends and peace reigns. In it reside your fulfillment, riches and power. In that core is your light, your 'word,' and your whole, sexy sacred self.

Awareness underpins your essence and being. Your emptiness is not empty. It's filled with your undiscovered magnificence. Don't get stuck in the words. Words only point at essence; they are not essence. Let them float in the space of your being, and become aware of that space in you.

Everywhere

The internal awareness that's beyond health is everywhere within and without you. It's formless and has no inside or outside. You can't picture it. Some people call it the 'zero point field.' It's also been called peace, joy and love, as well as presence, perfection and ultimate reality. Some name it wholeness or consciousness. It can't be understood, but can be known. It's beyond, but also within your body, social group and nature. Actually, you belong to it. Awareness is your impersonal, infinite essence.

It's what you deep down long for and seek to be one with, and the cosmic joke is that it's already everywhere that's real, including inside your being. The only place where it's NOT is in your fantasies and your imagination. Its nature is sexy. If your awareness is disconnected from itself because you've focused it elsewhere, you miss the sexy nature of being aware of your internal essence.

Think about it this way. **Peace is already everywhere that's real, but only peace can perceive that**. Your foundation of peace is more powerful than anything else, and this power of peace is sexy. However, peace is so real that it can't exist in what's not real. What exactly is not real? All words, thoughts, theories, concepts, ideas and ideals are made up. Because they are mental constructs, they are neither real nor true. Peace is never found in them. Why so? Real peace, which exists only in reality, cannot exist in theory. Theoretical peace is an imagined mental construction. It is a mirage without substance. Two insights flow from the above statement about peace.

First, if you can't connect with the peace that is everywhere, it's because the focus of your awareness is not connected to the peace that exists within you, and the peace in you therefore does not inform your perception. When peace in you informs your looking, it sees peace everywhere. In fact, then all it sees is peace. Only **peace can see, hear and feel peace**. Know the peace YOU are in you, and you know the peace that's everywhere. Your state of being creates your reality. That's how it works. **Peace recognizing peace is sexy**.

Second: The fact that most of us don't know the peace that is everywhere indicates the extent to which we live our lives in fantasy. Recent research shows that you notice only 10% of what goes on in the world, even when you pay attention to it. 90% of what you report isn't happening in the outside world, but you project it onto the outside world from your memories, beliefs and prejudices, and from your attitudes and your imagination. Though you hold these to be true in your mind, they're figments, illusions or delusions that you substitute for truth. Some people even call them personal hallucinations. Not real, they're not sexy. **Real is really sexy**.

Most of us live much of our lives in mental constructs that have no basis in reality. Most of our problems come from living that way. It's a scary thought. It'd be REALLY scary if it weren't for the presence enlightened souls living on our planet who know better. They help us re-focus our awareness into reality as soon as we realize our need to do so. **Life is sexy**.

This, in a variety of different words, is the message of great masters, the sexiest human beings to grace this planet with their presence.

They and their messages were so sexy that many of you are still in love with them, even hundreds or thousands of years after their physical departure. **Masters are sexy and mastery is sexy.** One of them, Socrates, said, "Know thyself!" He also said, "The unexamined life is not worth living." Jesus said, "You will know the truth, and the truth will make you free." He also said that there is a "peace that passes all understanding," and a "perfect love that casts out all fear." Masters have said, "I am in you, as you are in me." And "You and I are one."

A wise man knows that peace is every person's greatest personal achievement. From what is now known about life, biology, inner experience and the nature of the universe, I can assert and confirm that all of you can live your lives lit up from within. The light of life is in all of you, and when you look deeply enough into that light, you embody it. The master you seek is the life within you. It's sexy. Look! The internal master's sole agenda is to unconditionally care for you through all your dramas and traumas. That master never steers you wrong. **Knowing that master is sexy.**

In fact, what most people call 'sexy' today is what, in other times and other cultures, was called 'holy', 'sacred', 'inspired' and 'enlightened'. Sexy is more about being present to life than it is about the sexual act, although it includes that, too.

Live in harmony with the inner master. It's the best way to live. You radiate light, peace and sexy all at the same time. Feeling whole, fulfilled and cared for comes from living lit up from within. You feel so real and rich that it becomes easy to live in harmony with other people. Feeling cared for by life, you're free to make sure that the basic needs of all are met. That makes the world sexy. If you're like me, you can hardly wait to make your sexy contribution to manifest that sexy world.

Indestructible

Beyond Health is what's formless, indestructible, everywhere present and self-aware. Beyond Health cannot sicken, get old or perish. What has no form to begin with cannot be destroyed.

Indestructible is solid and thus without fear. **Indestructible is sexy**. Your body has form and is subject to breakdown. It can be repaired but will one day break down beyond repair. Your thoughts have form, but continue to change as you think about things in the face of changing contexts. You change your mind a lot. The world you live in has form, and everything constantly changes. Seasons and vegetation change, the weather is different every day, and tides ebb and flow. Night follows day. The moon waxes and wanes. Waterways dry up at times and flood at times. Earth moves under your feet.

Because they have form, your body, mind and nature can break down. This makes their charm short-lived. Subject to breakdown, creatures are subject to fear. You fear loss of your form, and you also fear losing something or someone that has a form to which you have become emotionally attached. You know that you must lose it eventually, but you don't want to lose it. You fight the inevitable. That's not sexy.

Wise people don't fight but accept what is, as it is. Your expectation that nature should run its course in a way that suits your delusions detracts from your sexiness. **It's sexy to enjoy life as it is**. It's not sexy to fear the inevitable death of the physical body. Live in your temporary body aware of the permanent peace that is its foundation.

The indestructible is present within your temporary breakdown-prone body and mind. You can choose to focus on the future of your body, which creates anxiety. You can try to rigidly hold to ideas without changing them in the light of new facts and contexts, but this kind of stubborn resistance is tedious to be around and is not sexy. Or you can, while living in a changing body and with a changing mind, keep your focus also on what is changeless and indestructible in your being.

Aware of the indestructible foundation of your being, you can navigate the changing world with equanimity. Don't get lost in changes by giving them more importance than they merit. **Equanimity is sexy**.

Real

You know Beyond Health only by experience. It is the union of awareness with your source. You cannot know the nature of what is beyond health in symbolic, imagined or belief-based ways. It has no existence in your mind, because mental constructs are not real, and Beyond Health exists only in reality. **Real is sexy**. Awareness is YOUR essential nature. Awareness is unlimited, existing inside and outside you, with no break between the center *in here* and its infinite expansion *out here*. It's who everyone, in basic essence, is. All of us are single points in that awareness.

This raw experience of vastness, which is impossible to disturb, is calm and sexy peace. Sexy is not men flexing their muscles and prancing around showing them off. Sexy is not women flaunting their assets. Sexy is calm presence in both genders, fully and comfortably present into their deepest being as well as their changing mind and body. That's *'wow' sexy*.

Your calm presence is a finely balanced line midway between bragging with bravado and hiding with shame. Sexy is not something you can put on from the outside with powders, fragrances, liners and colors. It's something that naturally shows up when you fully occupy or inhabit the being you are, which lights up your physical existence as well.

The magnificence of full presence in all of your being cannot be overstated. You can breathe your way toward it, but it is beyond breath. Real is an experience available to every human being at any time. The fact that you are a center of life within a mental framework, within a physical body, within a social group, within a natural environment, on a planet within a solar system, within a galaxy, within timeless infinity is awesome to experience and know. That's sexy.

I'm not talking about something you can take a 'selfie' photo of using your cell phone and show off to friends. You can't make a drawing of it. Words don't create this reality. You won't see or hear it on the evening news. This reality shows up only after you've let go of words by taking your awareness out of the mental realm. The concepts, theories and belief systems we create, invent and imagine into being have nothing true or real to them. Of themselves, they're nothing. Before you disagree, bear with me and consider what I'm saying for a few more moments. You can chuck it later.

You think of thoughts and ideas as things, but they are not. This is true even for ideas 'whose time has come'. However, when you dedicate the power of your life to an idea and commit your body to actions to create a physical reality in the shape of that idea, then you create something real out of an idea that is itself alone, not real.

Let me say it another way. Ideas have no power or reality to them. Your life is power, and your body is its instrument. When you apply both the power of the life you are and the instrument of your body to an idea, you can create a new reality that resembles that idea. It took me a while to 'get' that ideas are not real. Once I got it, it empowered me immensely.

If ideas, theories and beliefs are not real, you're free to make them up any way you want, from nothing, from scratch. None of them will be real. But you can use your life and body to create a reality in line with them. Why not make up ideas that, when you dedicate your life and body to them, manifest a sexier world than the one into which you were born, cultured and educated?

You might as well make it global and heartfelt, and create it in a way that serves all lives including yours on the planet, rather than just your life and the lives of a few of your buddies, tribe members and friends at the expense of everyone else.

This is how you can create new worlds and possibilities that work better for all. The formless reality that exists in each of us contains all possibilities. Anything is possible. That's super-sexy.

Quench That Thirst

You experience the infinite in quiet solitude. It's what your heart longs for and needs. Quench the thirst of your heart to be one with your source and feel that oneness in the core within the depth of your being.

Remarkably, there is in you a longing, want and thirst to know the boundless within you. Many words are used to name that longing. I'll post many of the words I've heard people use to name that inner longing to know the deepest secret, as well as words they use for what they're longing for on www. totalsexyhealth.com.

At 17 years old, I remember feeling pain in my chest. I had no explanation for it because it was not then a topic of common discussion. Looking back, I know that it began much earlier, but the distractions I focused on to obscure that pain ran out when I was 17, and blaming my pain on people and situations no longer worked. I could no longer shake the feeling. Despite deliberately looking for answers, it eluded me for another 13 years.

I had no idea that this was my heart (core) calling my awareness to come back home inside to life. Eventually, a teenager told me, "The peace you search for in the world is within you, and I can reveal you that peace." I had my doubts because I thought I knew quite a lot about life and living. But having experienced the big war in Europe, peace was important to me, so I decided to take him up on his offer.

Long story short, in 1972 I began a practice of taking time every day for solitude to explore and get to know the inner nature of my being. It completely changed my life from one of fearful and anxious war baby to a most amazingly and unconditionally-loved-by-life baby. I've re-written my life story from the perspective of the personal experience of life's unconditional love for me, and that new story has replaced most of my war baby story. That's a sexy transformation.

A few years ago, I was thinking back on my life's journey, and my retrospect became one of my favorite projects: **THIRST OF THE HEART**: The Most Important NOT Had Conversation In The World. In this interactive conversation, I ask participants about 30 questions, and each one answers every question. It takes about 2 hours. You'll find more on this conversation at www.totalsexyhealth.com.

I want to have this conversation with 8 billion people. **Acknowledgment of the thirst of the heart is sexy**. It is a powerful starting point for finding your life's central anchor.

Many of the thousands of people with whom I've had this conversation told me it was life changing for them, in the best possible way. I've met no one who could not identify his or her thirst of the heart feeling. People have different names for it, but all know it. Hardly anyone knows what to do with it. Not sexy. Imagine that! We don't know what to do with the core question of existence. That question has a powerful personal answer. Thirst of the heart is a huge gift because it calls and nags you to keep coming back to the central question of existence until you find the experiential answer to it. When you heed the call and do the work, you find your sexy core.

Historically, most people have lived and died with this central question unanswered. Not sexy. The intensity of that feeling drives most of your creative and destructive activities. When you address the thirst of the heart, you continue to be as creative as ever or even more so, and you become much less destructive. That's sexy.

The thirst of the heart conversation is the starting point for the changes that we need to make in how we live together sustainably as individuals in our natural environment. It's a potent conversation. Let me know when you want to have it. Quenching the thirst of your heart is super-sexy.

All

The personal experience of an infinite foundation is attractive and sexy. It can be called the 'All,' but many different names refer to it. The deepest desire and longing of every being is to know and be one with our infinite, mysterious, invisible source.

Someone once called it the 'ocean of answers'. That ocean is filled with answers for which you've not even formulated questions yet. Endless answers float in that ocean. In fact, all your questions dissolve in the internal ocean of answers, not because they're answered in a specific verbal way, but because in your central state of being, you are not confused about life and living. You're filled with joy and wonder at the magnificence of your existence. What's to ask when there's enjoyment? **The internal ocean of answers is sexy.**

You'll notice that when you tap into that internal presence, you'll also get new insights into any topic you focus on. It's a place of unlimited knowledge embedded in life. Where else should you find the answers about life and living than within the life that creates you and your living world? Whatever is your area of interest, you find simple, practical, profound understanding of that area when you connect your awareness to what is deeper than health within you.

In that state, there are no thoughts because it is beyond how deep thoughts can take you. Insights from there are not the result of thinking something through. They're already present in that state, and show up the moment you present a topic to the ocean of answers. They're natural answers based on the nature of reality.

Imagine having unlimited resources that you can apply to whatever question, problem, challenge, or interest you have. All that's within you. To dig it out, spend time alone, still, relaxed with your awareness on the thirst of the heart. Feel it. Sit with it. It may feel intense, but it will not hurt or eat you. Don't judge it. Just feel it. Accept it. Acknowledge it. Embrace it. Learn to appreciate and even be grateful for it, because it is your greatest gift other than being alive. That ache will lead you to the open door within your core through which you enter the boundless mansion of your being.

Be patient. Expect that it may take time and practice to get good at bringing awareness back to the center of your being. For decades, you've focused your awareness on your thoughts, your body or the outside world, and you've spent little, if any, time with your awareness immersed in the ocean of answers that is your deeper inner being. You get good at what you practice, so commit to and practice focused inward concentration. With time, you'll get as good at bringing your awareness inside as you've become at moving awareness outward. Within, you get to know your brilliant self.

In your awareness, you can be present in the peace that is real, knowable and beyond health, but also present in your body and the world. How present are you? The answer depends on your practice of presence on a moment-to-moment basis. When you have that experience, you are one with all that is.

In that experience, each one of you is fully home, fully accepted and fully welcome. Letting go, you can enter this state of peace. The moment you create an agenda, the focus of your awareness shifts from oneness to that agenda, and you'll likely lose your connection with oneness. It's not easy to be one with infinity and at the same time be preoccupied with your manufactured separate self.

The realm of oneness is the only realm in which misuse is not possible. What do I mean? Let me give an example. A terrorist can learn and improve mental skills and how to eat and work out more effectively, thereby becoming a more effective terrorist. The feeling of oneness cannot be misused, because when you misuse it, YOU lose your experience of it. It's instant payback.

Be self-aware. Internal self-awareness is your greatest gift to yourself and to the world.

2

PERFECT HEALTH:
Life, Light, Energy

Unconditional Catalyst

LIFE IS THE SECOND KEY part of total sexy health designed by nature. Life energy, which is perfect health, is perfectly sexy. Why is life perfect health? Life is energy in formless flow. It can't be created or destroyed. Energy feels no pain, never gets sick, and does not degenerate. Life energy is beyond death. As life, you are beyond all these. You are life, and life is whole. How do you know? You know it when you focus your awareness into life.

Your body, having form, is subject to breakdown. You feel pain, get sick or injured, and show symptoms of breakdown. Energy never shows deficiency symptoms. It is always perfectly healthy. Energy cannot be poisoned. It cannot be cut, dehydrated or starved. It has no eyelids and needs neither rest nor sleep. It is not made stronger by exercise or activity. It needs no food to power it because power is its nature. As perfect health, life energy is perfectly sexy.

Before going on, let me share a story that points to how we

confuse life and the body in our assessments and our use of words. When we look at people, we judge them to be sexy or not on the basis of their physical endowments. We talk that way to friends in our casual conversations. Like it or not, it's a learned cultural habit.

But sometimes, the one whose bodily endowments we so admire dies. First, we're in shock. As soon as we recover from it, we notice that his/her body is no longer attractive to us. The body has not changed. It's the same, only now it is life-less. Maybe we don't even want to look at it or touch it. Maybe we want to get away from it. We call someone and have it taken away. Within a few days, we bury or burn that body we so loved, or we get others to do it for us. So let me ask you a question. When you love a person, is it life or the body that you love? If you say both, then why don't you keep the body around when the life is gone?

Life keeps your body going all the time, regardless of whether you forget, ignore or even curse it. Life cares for your body without asking anything in return. While you wake and sleep, life beats your heart, moves your breath in and out, and digests your foods. It repairs your injuries. Life's unconditional love for your body makes life your body's perfect lover.

Life integrates the events of the day with your internal mental maps of yourself in the world, your personality. Life makes thinking possible. You get to choose your thoughts. A friend and mentor said it well, "The ability to think is life's gift to you. What you think about is your gift to yourself."

Life is a catalyst. What is that? A catalyst enables something to happen but is not itself changed or affected by what it makes happen. Life is the catalyst that creates your DNA program of 20,000+ genes. It powers the transcription of your genes into the RNA program from which, in your cells, life makes structural proteins, functional enzymes and receptors. Life powers all of the chemical reactions that govern the entire biochemistry of body construction, repair of parts worn out, and removal of molecular debris resulting from all of these activities. As a catalyst, life makes possible the activities of

- Ingesting fresh building blocks in the form of food when more of them are needed
- Imbibing the water necessary for body functions when your body is thirsty for it
- Breathing to bring in air when your body needs oxygen for energy production
- Relieve your body of wastes in a full bladder or colon
- Going to bed to take rest and get sleep when your body is tired
- Putting on clothes when your body feels cold and taking them off when your body feels hot
- Moving your body away from what can hurt it
- Assessing what to fight or run from and what to embrace
- Perpetuating its game of physical embodiment
- Building shelter and safety for your body and those of others close to you
- Protecting and raising your offspring
- Playing games and doing work

Life catalyzes everything that makes possible the super-complex dance on all levels of physical existence and mental function, from electron movement to mass marches.

The Power That Is Life

Your life is the power that runs everything and remains unaffected by what it powers. In your personal essence, you are this energy, this power. Most of the time, you think of yourself as your physical body or as the stories and beliefs that you hold to be true. But, you are NOT your body. You say, "This is my body, my eyes, my arms and legs, my stomach, my neck, my feet and so on." 'My' is possessive, and means that you own the body and its parts. You are not your body. You are its owner.

You are NOT your thoughts, either. You call them 'my' thoughts, or 'my' brilliant insights. You own all of these mental capacities. You talk about my clothes, my bed, my house, my property, my neighborhood, my city, my province and my country. You're not any of these; they are your possessions. You are their owner. Most of the time, you don't pay attention to how imprecisely you use words. You don't notice how much confusion in understanding and communication comes from this lack of precision.

You're not your body or any of its parts. You are not any of your thoughts, images or stories. You're not any of what you cover your body with, nor are you what surrounds it. Nor are you a victim or slave of any of these.

If you aren't any of these, then what exactly are you? Think about it for a moment. If you strip away everything you are not, what is there that you cannot strip away? Is it a good question? I love this question. You can strip away clothing, home and environment. You can change your mind at will. You can lose arms, legs and body parts, and still be 'you'. You finally come down to what? One step up from unbroken infinite awareness, you are life. Beyond life is awareness, which is not personal (you), but universal (all).

Awareness owns life, and life owns the body. Life is the 'I' that owns your body. Your body is life's body. Life is the personal presence and power that you are. As life, you own and direct everything going on in your sphere of influence: your body, thoughts, words and actions, and their results, effects and consequences.

Contrary to modern materialistic science, energy has always preceded and 'owned' matter. The energy of the 'Big Bang' preceded the creation of matter and the galaxies made from it. Sunshine energy first activated and energized atoms on earth to power the chemical reactions that created molecules, which eventually led to the construction of biological creatures. At first meeting, a spark of energy that passes between two people precedes courtship, mating, pregnancy and physical embodiment.

This is also true regarding banks and money. Energy preceded their invention and still owns them both. Without life energy, banks and money have no meaning. Energy's supremacy also applies to business enterprises. Life energy precedes thinking and imagination, which in turn precedes their materialization into a business venture. No life; no inspiration; no business manifestation. Energy also precedes laws and government institutions, as well as the enforcement structures of courts and jails. Dead people need and make no laws. Bodies without life energy are not subject to enforcement or punishment, either.

In practice, most of us are rarely aware of the energy we are. Much of what we, as life, do in our body remains outside of our awareness. We don't focus on the energy-driven processes taking place within our cells, tissues and body systems. We take them for granted. Is it possible to become more energy-aware of these? Some people say we can. The extraordinary skills that some yogis master and some sages describe may be indicators of this possibility. Most of us don't aspire to be aware on that deeper level. We focus on the more obvious, largely external energy reflections off the surfaces of things with which we interact.

As life, you're each the king or queen of your domain. As life, you're each the master of your world. As life, you're the power that invents goals, and manifests outcomes and destinations. As life, you define the direction and limitations of your journey and the steps you take toward your destiny. It's part of the power of the life you are. But there's much more.

The more deeply aware you are of life, the more clearly you recognize the power that you are and how much you have been given. This is just one reason why wise teachers and masters recommend that you invest time every day in voluntary solitude to become more deeply aware of life as well as of awareness. Everything you've ever deep down wanted is already present in, or made possible by, these two realms: awareness and life.

Weightless

Life, the energy that powers every human being and other creature, is weightless and immaterial, but not unimportant. Without it, everything physical and mental breaks down, and you lose the integrity of your form. When life and body part company, the true nature of the body shows up. It is a shell of molecules that houses the power-filled flow of energy you are. When the house that is your body goes dark, it becomes useless and irrevocably disintegrates.

What is truly real about you as an individual? Life, which weighs nothing, and which you perceive only indirectly through its ability to move your body and enable you to think, is powerful. Your body is inert. Weightless life energy can make another body, but without life your body can make neither a life nor another body.

I've said it before. Life weighs nothing but runs everything. When your body is alive (which means: with life), almost anything is possible. Without life, nothing is possible, even if the physical body remains intact. This can happen, for instance, when a person is immersed in cold water for too long, and dies. The body remains intact, but when the weightless energy of life separates from it, it's over. I'll return to the topic of death in a later chapter.

What happens to the weightless energy of life at the point of death? That energy remains weightless and becomes physically invisible because you no longer notice its power translated into physical movement or the mental and emotional expressions that you can observe with physical senses. The body was never life when it was 'with life', and can never be life or awareness. Awareness and life both leave when life and the body separate. Where do they go?

In our present-day super materialistic world, this is a controversial topic. Here's what we know. After death, the structured arrangement of atoms and molecules that is the body breaks apart, and every atom in your body returns to the ground, air and water from which life took it. It's common sense.

It's also logical that life energy and awareness persist. Why do you think that the energy of life, which is non-material but real, would after separation from the body cease to be real? It's simply not true to the nature of things. A drop of water merges in the ocean. The atoms of the body merge with the soil. Gas merges with the atmosphere. The energy of life becomes part of the energy of the universe. Awareness remains in the infinite 'field' of awareness. Nothing is lost. Nothing that is real can become unreal.

What is life in you will always be life. What is aware will always be aware. Members of some cultures and traditions acknowledge and give expression to the presence of their 'ancestors', who are always present in essence, but without physical form. You cannot touch them, and they won't answer back, but your life is one with their life, and pure awareness in you is one with their essence of pure awareness.

To be fully aware of life within you is to be one with your weightless, indestructible, wise power. What will this add to your life? Something in you aches to know. Find out. You'll be pleasantly rewarded by richness, wholeness and fulfillment in the direct experience of life. Something in you has been seeking it since childhood. It's been calling you from within, nagging and begging you to bring your awareness back home to life.

Senses

Your senses perceive and measure energy because energy is the power that creates incessant change in the physical world. Using your senses, life monitors these changes to alert you to threats and invitations. **Being alert to your surroundings is sexy.**

Sexy life looks through your eyes and sees shapes, colors and movement. These are energy impressions from the world within which your body lives. Specifically, they are the difference between sunlight energy absorbed and energy reflected by the surfaces of things in your physical surroundings. Your sexy life looks and sees, knows that it sees, and uses your eyes as the instruments through which it sees. Without the perfect health of life, perfectly healthy eyes are blind.

Sexy life listens through your ears and hears silence broken by the energy of sounds that movement, activity and life produce. It is life, not your ears, that listens and hears. Without life, perfectly functional ears are deaf and hear nothing.

Sexy life feels through your body, both internally and externally, the energy of pressure, pain, pleasure and gravity (position in space) that internal change and close-up activity and movement produce. It is life, not your body, which registers feelings. Without life, a perfectly formed body feels nothing.

Sexy life tastes through your tongue and registers blandness interrupted by the tastes of sweet, sour, bitter, salty, spicy and pungent that the interactions of different molecules with sensing pits in your tongue trigger. It's life, not the tongue that registers taste. Without life, a perfect tongue tastes nothing.

Sexy life smells through your nose, and registers odorless, fragrance-free air broken by tens of thousands of fragrances that air currents carry and you inhale when you breathe in through your nose. It is life, not your nose that detects odors. Without life, a perfectly structured nose smells nothing.

Your senses inform you of change in the outside world, but you mostly don't notice the inner light or sound within your body.

What would happen if you could look, listen, feel and taste inwardly? What would you discover? You'd discover the essence of sexy. The truth is that you CAN see, hear, feel and taste life when you answer your heart's longing, get still in solitude and focus your attention within. If you want to do that exploration (which is sexy), and you practice it long enough to become good at it, you find that in the darkness within your being there is sexy light. In the silence within you, there is sexy sound. In the emptiness within your core, there is sexy feeling. In the blandness in your tongue, there is sexy sweetness. **In your personal essence, you are that sexy light, that sexy sound, that sexy feeling and that sexy taste.**

Whole

Life, which is energy, which is light, sound, feeling and taste, is so whole that it can never break down, sicken or deteriorate. That's sexy. **Perfect health and energy is perfectly sexy.**

Fire cannot burn the energy of life. Wind can't blow it away. It can't be bent, spindled or mutilated. Water can't wet or freeze it. A sharp instrument can't cut it. A bullet cannot put a hole in it. A bomb can't blow it apart. In seeing, hearing and feeling the energy of life, you get to know a wholeness that's not physical.

All day and all night, without weekends or holidays off, life energy re-builds your body for an average of 75+ years. Your body, constantly being damaged and repaired, is a major 24/7/365 construction site. Life powers the removal and replacement of 98% of the atoms in your body each year, and draws in more than 12 times your body weight of water, washes your body with it internally and then removes it. Life also pulls about 3 times your weight of free oxygen into your body annually.

Wholeness is not physical. It's the feeling of life. Whole by nature, life does not depend on and remains unaffected by the state of your body, your mind, your tribe and your environment. That's sexy. Let's push this even further. Even when your body is racked with disease, your thinking is completely disorganized, your social group is in chaos and your environment is a disaster area, your life energy is not affected and you feel whole the moment that you focus your awareness into it.

Drama, trauma, crisis and emergency distract you from the feeling of wholeness in life. It's understandable that you should attend to them. But is it possible to attend to them and still maintain your connection with the whole feeling of life at the same time? Yes, it's possible. It's simple, but becomes easy only with practice. That's why wise ones recommend that you master re-connecting with the feeling of wholeness in life before crises distract you, while you have the time and luxury to do so.

The saying, "When you're up to your ass in alligators, it's hard to remember that your original intent was to drain the swamp," rings true, but it is 'hard' to remember, not impossible. May I tell you a story from childhood?

You already know that I was born in a war. As a child, I got completely caught up in the drama and trauma of it. All the while, life took perfect care of me from inside, but my awareness was focused on the external mess of war and social chaos.

It first occurred to me when I was 27 (24 years after the war ended) that life had cared for me through all of it, and then it struck to me that maybe I should make friends with and get to know this life that had so well looked after me. Soon after, I began to practice re-connecting my awareness inwardly to life. As I become better at doing so, I continue to be pleasantly amazed and surprised by the feeling of beauty embedded in life.

Now my practice of self-knowledge is easy and fun, and most days I look forward to doing it. Through this practice, I began to see my life from the perspective of life rather than that of war. In retrospect, I know that as scary as it was, the terror of being a child in a war was a powerful gift to me. Why?

If finding real peace and promoting the possibility of it is part of my purpose for being here, the best way to prepare for that mission is to learn early what happens when we don't cultivate peace when we have space and time for it!

Don't start your inner practice when you're fleeing from the guns of the wars that started because you did not give time to the practice of peace during peacetime. Start NOW. If enough individuals had done so, we could have pre-empted and prevented the Big War. If enough of you do so now, all wars can be ended and prevented.

Peace is both the cure and the prevention of war. And, peace is a personal, internal, real experience with roots within every single living human being. Before peace can take over the world, though, you have to let it take over your inner world of awareness.

Let me make one other point. There has never ever been anything wrong with any of you, no matter what others have told you or what you've told yourself. Nothing has ever been wrong with you, even though you disconnected from life, felt bad feelings, thought nasty thoughts, said hurtful words and acted destructively with predictable destructive results. How can that be? You are not your feelings, not your thoughts, not your words, not your actions and not their consequences.

In your essence, you are life and awareness, and there has never been, is not now, and can never be anything wrong with life or awareness. In your essence, you have always been whole, cared for and perfect. When you live aware of both life and awareness, you increasingly become an expression of these two perfections, and what you feel, think, say, and do changes in positive ways.

Rich

As life, you're fearless. You are courageous, powerful and independent. You are also real, full, generous and kind. You're rich, beautiful and true. You're light and sexy. When you know yourself as life, there's nothing missing. You've always been, are now, and will always be rich. Regardless of the shape of your body, mind, group or surroundings, you cannot be hurt, are rich and will never be anything but rich. That is the nature of the energy of life you are.

That's great news for each of the 8 billion people living here today. Everything that can fall apart will fall apart. Everything that can change will change. Everything that cannot change will not change. Unchangeable is the nature of life, which is perfect health. It's really sexy. You can ecstatically celebrate this, and celebration is sexy.

You are rich beyond belief. Life will never let you down. Every gadget and every person on whom you depend will let you down, but life won't let you down. Even in your darkest hour, life does not abandon you. In death, your body will fail to serve you but life, which is your essence, will be with you forever because it's what you are.

With life, you've been given everything. Life feels perfect. Life is reliable, far beyond your wildest dreams and your physical capacity. Life takes care of everything going on in your body. Life never complains, takes time off, or punishes you for not giving it attention or remembering it. It never charges for its unconditional love. It never asks for anything, gives everything and takes care of the smallest details. It holds you up and holds nothing back. Life fills you with light, enlightens you and makes you wise.

Life answers all your questions, is 100% for you, and has no agenda but to serve your body's needs and mind's desires. Life saves you when you mess up, and continues to care for you patiently when you're physically sick, mentally confused, judged by others or locked up. No matter how long and how far you've wandered away, life lets you come back to it the moment you want to come home, without any recrimination. Where else can you find that kind of non-judgmental acceptance?

With life, you have everything. As life, you own the world. You don't own it exclusively, or possessively, or forever. You own it for the moment, and for enjoyment. Has anyone ever been richer than you are? No, but how much of your inborn, life-given riches have you dug out and discovered so far? Life loaded you with sexy goodies, but it doesn't force you to enjoy any or all of them. You focus on and enjoy only as many as you want, when you want. Want more? Dig more. Happy? Enjoy. Whenever you're ready, there's a lot more for you to discover, get to know and enjoy.

On a wagon drawn by an old, tired horse, with a mother and six children fleeing from a war zone where no one is a friend, there's a child lit up by life in the midst of chaos. Rich beyond measure but not knowing this and therefore fearful and terrified, life holds him in its loving embrace, knowing he will survive, the flight will end and things will get better. This is life's promise and possibility for every human being. Once I 'got' it, I began to feel more grateful.

As life, you are the light in your body and the light in your world. How lit up are you and is your world? Your practice of going to and being the light you are determines how brightly you shine. As life, you're the unspeakable original word in your body and the word in your world. How present is the word in your world? The answer depends on your practice of inner listening. As life, you're the feeling of perfect wholeness in your body and your world. How whole is your world? The answer depends on how whole you feel within. It depends on your practice of being aware of the feeling of wholeness rooted within the life you are.

In that experience, I am perfect health in my world. When you are in that experience, you are perfect health in your world. In that experience, each one of us is fully whole, healthy and sexy.

You can't misuse the feeling of life. Heartless acts disconnect you from the feeling of life. I know this from experience. My heart hurts when I act in a mean and heartless way. The ache ends the moment I learn the lesson, resolve not to act that way again, make amends, and change my behavior. The heart ignores apologies. It responds to heartfelt behavior. I like myself best when I live with my awareness heart-centered.

Many people believe in punishing those who transgress the rules of human care and respect. There's a place for that. People deserve to be protected from those who mean to do them harm. Hopefully, transgressors get put in a place in which they can discover more of the inner beauty and care life has for them, which then catalyzes changes of their destructive behaviors to more constructive ones.

Some people believe, without real world evidence, that 'bad' people will be punished after they die. In truth, life punishes heartless behavior instantly. The moment you act heartlessly, you break your connection to the rich and cared for feeling in your heart. Instantly, you deprive yourself of feeling the most fulfilling feeling. You get to return to it after you make things right by giving up the heartless ideas in your mind that led to your heartless actions.

Regarding what you teach in the world, consider that most teaching is double-edged. Information may be used with equal effectiveness for constructive and for destructive ends. However, there is no potential down side of teaching oneness and connection into life.

Be present in your power. Be more fully present every day in the power that, as life, you are.

3

MENTAL HEALTH 1:
Inspiration, Creativity

Bridge

INSPIRATION IS THE THIRD KEY part of total sexy health designed by nature. Inspiration is the non-material bridge between your life and the world you live in, and leads to creativity. In fact, inspiration is the driving force behind vision and purpose. Inspired or energized by life, you create visions in your mind's eye, embody them for execution, and so manifest them into your world. Out of endless potential, you imagine into being what can create a happier, safer or more comfortable situation.

Inspiration is an experience of awareness of life from which anything is possible. From inspiration, you imagine new possibilities into being. Inspired, you create thriving.

Life-inspired, you are a creator. Out of formless awareness, you first create a mental form—picture, sound, feeling or thought—that has no substance. You enroll your body to translate it into physical form. Translation includes structures made of physical stuff such as wood, glass and metal, but can also be conceptual, institutional or social, like 'standard operating procedures' (SOPs), laws, logistics systems (for delivery of goods and services) and so on.

Look around you in any town or city. Everything you see that life made, using humans, involved inspired creativity. Not only the obviously big structures, but the little ones as well, such as nails and rivets, windowsills and doorframes, and paper clips and post-it notes. Through humans, life imagined books shelves, carpets and air vents into being. Bed sheets, mattresses, pillows, toilets and mirrors came from the gift of inspired creativity. Every part of pots, stoves, fridges and vacuum cleaners arose from life's inspired creative imagination. Trains, planes, cars and bicycles came from inspired creative minds. Life imagined roads, traffic signs and maps into being. Techno-gadgets and Internet came about, byte by byte, through the inspired creative imagination of thousands of nerds. Life induced millions of people over thousands of years to invest hundreds of trillions of hours in efforts to make the human journey better and safer. When you stop to think about it, it's both awesome and noble what life has brought about through inspired human creativity.

Life energy is even more awesomely creative and inspired in its biological designs. It produces the genius genetic blueprint that holds the necessary physical directions to build the molecules and complex infrastructures of all creatures' bodies, big and small. Life also creates brilliant biological systems that adapt different creatures to water, air or land, with glands and organs specialized for a long list of different tasks. Life builds the exquisitely integrated systems that repair, self-renew and reproduce cells and tissues. Life-built systems support individual lifespans that range from minutes to centuries, and the survival of species from brief seasons to hundreds of millions of years.

Life designs the senses, through which it connects you to the physical world of which your body is part. All that you sense–see, hear, feel, taste and smell–serves as the energetic bridges between your body and the physical world.

By its genius design of human beings, life's inspired creativity enables you to give form to possibilities. Out of the infinite potential that exists in formless awareness, you turn possibilities into plans, and then harness bodies to construct new realities that did not exist in nature.

Inspired *constructive* creativity makes physical existence more enjoyable and less painful. Inspired *destructive* creativity improves life for some at the expense of others. Dreamers, visionaries, poets, composers and storytellers are some of the people whose inspired creativity serves social growth and contribution. We admire such people. There's something sexy about living in imaginary worlds that have not yet been created, and being a source, director and active part of creating them.

Inspiration

The word: 'inspire' means 'to breathe in'. Breathing in, you get in touch with the energy of life. That energy is formless power, light and lightness. Experiencing your energy and insight, you can joyfully dream, imagine and invent anything into existence. What you specifically create depends on where you are, the company you keep, and what is needed.

The light you are delights in lighting up your world. You invent what'll bring more joy, hope and comfort, or less darkness and pain. You do it globally for all, or you do it locally for a few (family, club, nation, etc.).

Inspiration drives contribution. Feeling inspired, the mental constructs that limit you and get you stuck, evaporate. Inspiration fills your mental ruts with hope and power, which lift you up above them. What's considered normal and settled no longer stops you from dreaming up something even better.

Inspiration is a freer state of being. It untethers you to conceive something new, and releases your energy from the limitations of concepts, beliefs and rules that dampen freedom. With fewer limitations, you can do more things. The impossible becomes possible. **Inspiration is sexy**.

Inspiration organizes your entirety around a possibility. It's a magnificent obsession, an addiction to elevate people and the world. Inspiration is super-hot, electric and attractive to others. People love inspired company. They like to be close to and work in the aura of those inspired.

Inspiration defies logic. Inspiration is a high energy, god-like, felt passion. For better or worse, people follow those inspired, addicted to the connection, even if the goal is destructive. Many of the world's worst dictators began their journey as inspired leaders promising to improve affairs for their fellow citizens, but changed into monsters as time went on, sometimes leading their country to perdition. The most powerful politicians, business moguls, religious and cult leaders are inspired. Some of them lack empathy for and connection with those who are not part of their small flock of friends. They've failed to connect to the internal feeling of being cared for by life. They use their charisma to serve discontent egos and minds, and sometimes create a lot of trouble for themselves and the people who believe in them.

Even when it's destructive, inspiration is attractive. This makes inspiration dangerous when the goal is not to 'benefit all at the expense of none' (Buckminster Fuller). When inspiration is not connected to the internal foundation of contentment, it often leads to disastrous destinies.

History has recorded a long list of misdeeds and catastrophes engineered by inspired but heartless despots. Many such people presently live and occupy positions of great influence and power, without great wisdom. Which heartless, silver-tongued, corrupt influencers do you follow blindly? To which inspired despot or dictator do you give your power?

Your connection to your sexy inner voice of calm, heartfelt wisdom for living is more powerful than any outer source of corruption. When you cultivate it, it protects you from being tricked and victimized. How solid is your connection to the energy and light in your core that is your source of mental clarity? What sexy inspiration have you come up with, built on these? Does what you want to do bring benefit to all at no one else's cost? In daily practice, do you serve life, people and nature, or do you serve ideas, ideals, and bank accounts?

Create

Human beings are creative by nature. Life created us with a mind that enables us to think and even more special, to imagine. It's what makes us so creative. We use life's powerful gift of mind to develop thousands of lifesaving, work easing and time sparing conveniences. Before the advent of the human mind, such creations remained unknown in 4 billion years of nature.

Mind is also a powerful curse. In addition to our beneficial creations, we invented super-destructive gadgets and poisonous molecules. We deem these necessary only because we do not use our creativity to devise ways in which we all can be content and live in health and harmony together.

Creativity itself can also be a curse. Yesterday's breakthroughs become tomorrow's nightmares. Take fossil fuels, for instance. They made industry, air conditioning and self-powered vehicles possible. A century later, they result in climate change, the loss of species, extreme weather and pollution. While we can argue some points, one fact about fossil fuels cannot be argued. Each atom of carbon from coal, oil or 'natural' gas you burn takes two atoms of oxygen out of your breathing air. In Chapter 7, we talk about environmental health, and will continue this story.

Here are other examples. The fishing industry brought us food and raw materials, but decimated fish stocks in our oceans. Plastics enabled thousands of conveniences but now pollute our land and sea. Social rules keep groups together, but turn into sources of inter-group conflict. We learned to use salt to preserve meat and fish, but we cut down forests to create the fires that evaporate water to produce salt. That's what happened to the forests of England and other parts of Europe. In addition, high blood pressure and other health problems result from using so much of salt.

To use your inborn creativity constructively, you need a solid foundation in awareness and life energy. That's why all wisdom teachers advise that you make awareness of life your priority. It's why practicing self-knowledge to search, discover and connect to the magnificent foundation of your existence is so important. When you experience that with life you have everything, you're less tempted to exploit, cheat and kill to get more. Then you're no longer deluded to think you need to grab more stuff to feel full.

Instead, you feel good when you give what you have in excess of your basic needs to those who have less and need it. When you connect to 'source' and feel content, you change from taking more to giving more because you are full now and so have more to give. You do what needs to be done to serve life, instead of obsessively trying to fill your emptiness.

You can now use your personal interests, strengths and abilities, knowing the needs that exist in the world, to make the biggest splash for good. You now live into the needs of situations and circumstances in which you find yourself. That's sexy. People notice. What you do flows better. You become more creative and less destructive. Now, you can create inspired and inspiring thoughts and images, and transform them into realities that enhance life's innate abundance.

You can now think globally. Thinking big requires the same amount of effort as does thinking small. So why think small? Be a creator of global destinies. Now, no problem is too big to take on. Also, when you're solid in your foundation and an issue needs course correction, you're free to make that correction without resistance. You now know that your fulfillment does not depend on outside pursuits, but comes from awareness of your inner foundation.

Improve

Inspired within a solid foundation in awareness and life, it's normal and natural for you to use your creativity to upgrade quality of life as much as you can, for you, all others and all of nature.

Some people claim that happy and fulfilled people become lazy. That is in fact not true. I've seen it in my own life and in the lives of many others. Feeling fulfilled, you become clearer and therefore more productive because you're less filled with doubt. You use your time and your energy more effectively. You have more energy because you're not wasting it in confusion and doubt. You can work longer before you need a break or get tired. You interact better with people. You give clearer instructions, as you're clearer in your focus and understanding. You need less time off to pursue distractions. In finding the best plan of action, your selfishness gets in the way less. You appreciate the people you work with more. They appreciate you more back. As a result, you get more done.

When you work from joy rather than from fear, the results are better. Chasing carrots is more fun than running from whips. Inspiration and passion draw you forward. When you love what you do, you look forward to working, stay late when necessary and go home proud of your day's effort and accomplishments. You come up with ways to make the workflow more effective and efficient. You innovate solutions and create better systems. In contrast, unhappy people cut corners, hide problems, tell lies, and do the least work necessary to keep their job.

As you get to know the light you are more deeply, you become a light that inspires other people to shine brighter. You become the light at the center of your sphere of influence. It makes you an exemplary leader, which is sexy. Lit up people are sexy. They bring light into darkness, and illuminate the world around them.

Light drives creativity, effort and work. Light inspires vision and originality. Nothing is impossible in light. Every issue in the world is made better by more light, more heart and more creativity. Throwing money at a problem will not solve it unless heart goes with the money. Even without money, more heart improves problems and leads to solutions.

As you know, money without heart can lead to great destruction. The head terrorists are rich people. Only those with extra cash (or credit) initiate the expensive national games of war and destruction. Money-hungry profiteers lay claim to Earth's natural resources and sell them back to us for profit only because they have a lot of money to begin with. Present and past religious groups that organize persecutions, inquisitions and witch-hunts, and who hide or protect abusers and molesters have power, position, privilege and money.

What needs to happen in the world will not happen through governments, religions, big business or other institutions. These are more the problem than the solution to global issues. Entrenched, outdated positions and views are a large part of what's wrong, has been wrong for ages, and has never been righted. The changes the world needs will come from individuals (including wealthy and powerful ones) who find their inner core and foundation. Such people live with inspired passion, and enthusiastically bust their butts to create a better, kinder, more harmonious world. You can be one such individual, in spite of entrenched, outdated and ineffective institutions.

Hope

Every inspired human being is creative. It's an inherent part of the life you come into the world loaded with. You're creative in countless personal, private and exclusive ways, in lofty, global and inclusive ways, and in constructive and destructive ways. You're not a robot who does as s/he's told. You're always experimenting.

With your foundation in awareness and life, and in touch with your inspired creativity and the world, you can be a source of hope for enriched, empowered and compelling futures for millions of people. It gives you reason to bounce out of bed in the morning, and it gives others reason to do the same.

The light that is your life is your great source of hope because in your direct knowledge of it, you feel worthwhile, whole and sexy. The meaning of life is in the experience of life. Life cares perfectly for you, me and every other human being every moment of every day. When you feel cared for by life, your inspired natural inclination is to help others up. All that's left to do is to extend a hand to those who don't yet feel that way, and to confidently address arising needs.

It's not complicated. Lit up, we're better together. Life is the worthy cause. Nature gives us all the necessary resources. You and I share what we don't need. Generosity comes not from deprivation and sacrifice, but from feeling content and cared for.

No obstacle keeps this from happening, except for discontent-based scarcity thinking. Since everything you think is made up, and you're free to make up whatever you want, why not make up thoughts that work for all? Why not think 'us all inclusive', globally? Why not deliberately focus your thinking on protection, care and enjoyment of life, body and nature?

When you lose touch with life, you lose your inspired creativity, lose hope, and easily fall into dark, negative and depressed self-destruction. "Without a vision, the people perish."

Life created your brain and mind as its computer. If you listen to life, you notice that life gives your brain and mind instructions to protect, serve and care. Life defines sanity that way. Any other use of your brain and mind is insane from life's perspective.

By life's definition, most human beings think, speak and act insane much of the time. Pay attention to your thoughts for 24 hours. Count how many of your thoughts, words and actions uplift, and how many demean and hurt. Include your put-downs of others not included in your groups when you're with friends. You may be surprised, shocked and even dismayed.

When you connect to awareness and the feeling of life, disciplining your creative mind to life's definition of sanity is easy. Without that connection, disciplining your mind is almost impossible. As your first priority, connect to awareness and the direct inner experience of your life. Build what's inspired, required and creative on that foundation.

Balance

I am the source of inspired creativity in my world, my personal sphere of influence. You are the source of inspired creativity in your world, YOUR sphere of influence. Large or small, each of us is the center of a personal sphere of influence.

Your degree of *total sexy health* measures to what extent you live fully present in all of your being. You are an example that elevates others or lets them down. Your state of being always affects those in your sphere of influence to become more like you. How do you show up in your being?

You model your state of being for others, and set an example, not only by your words but also by the actions that express it. You model the level of awareness (or ignorance) at your center. You model the inner light shining (bright or dim) from within. You model constructive or destructive creativity from inside yourself. You model physical health and habits from inward out. You model crisis management from your state of being. You model social behavior from your personal presence. You model relationship to nature out of yourself. You model oneness with the infinite scheme of things from inner relaxation. You model calm or agitated states of being from within you.

All of these together create your influence on self and the world. When all of these in you are in balance and you give each its due, you bring balance into your sphere of influence. **Balance is sexy.** Lack of balance in you shows up in your surroundings. Research shows that the ONLY reliable indicator of insightful living is the extent to which a person cultivates and deepens their inner experience.

As you align more closely with all of nature and your nature, you change your influence on your surroundings. Become more aware and disciplined through deepening self-knowledge. Become more positive by connecting to the light you are and the creativity that life inspires. Become more deeply aware of the infinite that orchestrates everything everywhere in this eternal moment. Powerfully affect your sphere of influence.

Like it or not, in your sphere of influence, you are the leader. Every other human being is the leader in her/his sphere of influence. To what do you lead? What do you model? You're free to influence those in your sphere in any direction you want. Be deliberate. Be aware. You have the power to make real the most remarkable world that you and humanity have ever dreamed of.

What some people have called 'Heaven on Earth' is possible. Some call it the 'Golden Age'. Those states of being already exist here. They've always been here. They're based on each individual's full and sexy presence. Some people already live aligned with that world. You don't need to wait for someone else to bring it. You can create it out of its existence in your nature. You can be the change, and create a world that in every way works for all, beginning with you. It's sexy to live that way.

Have you noticed that when you focus too much on change, you create stress in your mind, which can throw you off balance? Then you lose touch with your creative juices and become a victim of stress. You don't need to let that happen. Balance times of mental stress with inspired creative projects. Focus on dreams you want to develop. They keep your hope up. In the midst of stress, deliberately make time and room for creative projects.

Creativity keeps you light and restores your balance. Balanced, you deal with stress much better.

4

PHYSICAL HEALTH:
Fitness, Food & More

Context

YOUR BODY–FITNESS, FOOD AND MORE–IS the fourth key part of total sexy health designed by nature. But let's begin with a slightly larger context. As life, you're creator and instructor on how to use your body. As body, you're a vehicle for action to serve life in the world. As life, you're the 'determinator' of what to feed and how to exercise that body in ways that optimize its capacity to serve. As body, you're a physical contraption that life uses to protect and care for living human forms. Your body is life's physical instrument.

Life creates and moves your body around, and uses your body to move things around. Life creates your brain, and uses your brain and mind as its computer to absorb and process information, and to enable decisions that set the direction for work. Your body is your means for physical action on the physical plane of a physical planet.

Your first and most important activity is breathing. Breath is the bridge that links life with your body. When breathing stops, life and your body part company. Be aware of your breathing. It's the foundation of all your other physical doing. **Breathing is sexy**. On the bridge of breath, you cross from body awareness to life awareness, which reveals to you the power as well as the light you are. On the bridge of breath, you cross from life awareness to awareness of the body, your temporary physical 'machine'.

Physical health is a worthwhile but losing proposition. In time, your body gets diseased and demolished. This means two things. <u>First</u>, choose worthwhile projects. Uplifting, noble, inspired, empowering projects always involve caring for life. Don't squander your only body on trivial pursuits.

<u>Second</u>, don't be too attached to your body. Treat it like a good servant. Don't neglect it. Neglect is cruel, and that's not sexy. Don't indulge it. Indulgence is sloppy, which also is not sexy. When you treat your body with respect, it serves you effectively to accomplish worthwhile purposes for the longest possible time, with a minimum of pain. That's sexy. Eventually, as life, you give your used up, spent, exhausted body back to nature for recycling.

Physical pain results from different ways of living out of line with your surroundings, as when you

- Take in dirty air, water and food

- Bang into things

- Fight at times when you should run

- Act carelessly regarding dangers that sun, air, water and rocks can pose

- Allow toxins and damaged food molecules into your body

Toxic substances act like monkey wrenches in the biochemical architecture of your cells and tissues. They derail or block natural molecular interactions, produce symptoms of illness, and hasten your premature departure from your body. These include pesticides, plastics, drugs and industrial chemicals, but also cosmetics, preservatives and food molecules changed by industrial processing and food preparation. Oils damaged by heat during processing or cooking cause more health problems than any other part of nutrition. If you want physical health, don't fry, deep-fry or barbecue.

Life invented pain to get your attention, let you know that something needs to change, and push you in search of relief. When you make the necessary changes, healing happens, and then pain subsides and ends. If you don't respond to low-grade pain, life turns up the volume. Sooner or later, life will get your attention. If a grain of sand fails to alert you when you're not paying attention, life sends a rock. If a rock doesn't get your attention, life will send a boulder. Be alert. Avoid having a boulder wake you up.

Your body is made from sunlight, oxygen, water and food. That's it. For most of the time that our planet has been spinning in space, nothing else was required. Sun, air, water and foods properly used were primary health care. No drugs were needed. No drugs were used. To call the medical industry's service 'primary health care' misrepresents that service, which honestly is 'disease management'. This has a place, but let's call it what it is. Misrepresentation is not sexy. It creates confusion. It makes choosing health difficult, if not impossible.

Even preventive medicine is still disease-oriented. We use it to stave off cardiovascular disease, cancer, diabetes, arthritis, stroke and others. Why not go a step further and chase health instead? **Self-responsible health care is sexy**!!! Do you know why hardly anyone pursues health? Do you know why you don't pursue it? You don't know what to do to go to health. The people who tell you to be more responsible for your health don't provide you with a road map.

One hundred billion people have lived on planet Earth. None in all that time developed a clear, comprehensive definition of health or a true health care system. As a result, you lack the knowledge you need to make choices that bring you closer to total sexy health. This book provides an overview of tools for self-responsible health care. A definition of total sexy health must take nature and your human nature into account because that's where total sexy health lives. **Life invented total sexy health in nature and human nature.** When you give each key part of nature and your nature its due, you improve your 'sexy', one part at a time.

True primary physical health care, which makes you exude physical sexy, is the use of:

- Fitness, consisting of activity, recovery, rest and sleep
- Sunlight
- Fresh air (oxygen)
- Fresh water
- Fresh whole raw organic mostly plant-based foods
- Optimized digestion
- Avoidance of poisons and detoxification

Using all of these together, you create a body that works, repair a body that doesn't, and make your body optimally sexy. **Living with your body in line with nature is sexy.** Out of line with nature, you get sick. You can remedy most sicknesses by bringing your body back in line with nature and your nature.

Fitness

Fit is sexy. Your body is made for activity. If there's nothing to do, you don't need a body. Then you can be a disembodied spirit floating about in the 'ethers.' No matter how well you eat, inactivity breaks down your body, and activity builds it up.

You already know that you need a body for physical actions. We're always *schlepping* stuff from here to there and back again. Externally, you walk, run, jump and dance. You fight, flee and withdraw from danger. You explore. You build and tear down. You meet, sniff, embrace, mate and raise offspring. Internally, the body's 'doing' includes building, maintaining and repairing all cells, tissues, glands, organs and systems. And it includes your thinking, musing, and speaking. **Activity is sexy.**

You can't be incessantly active. Taking care of your body requires a balance between doing and resting. During times of rest and recovery, life rebuilds and heals your body. In addition to rest, you need sleep, for physical healing and for integrating the events of your day in a way that maintains the coherence of your personality. **Recovery, rest and sleep are sexy.**

Optimized intake of essential nutrients (18 minerals, 13 vitamins, 8 amino acids, 2 fatty acids) helps fitness. Among essential nutrients, undamaged omega-3, vitamin D and magnesium are most often too low for optimum health. Optimizing digestion also helps healing. If you cook foods, replace the probiotics and digestive enzymes that cooking destroys. Eat more plant-based fiber also.

Make sure that circulation is optimal. It is vitally important for health. Besides exercise, bioelectric 'fields,' healing touch, massage, chiropractic manipulation, relaxation, yoga, parasympathetic stimulation, and anything else that improves circulation helps healing and fitness.

Optimum fitness requires three kinds of activity: **endurance** activities such as running, biking and swimming for cardiovascular fitness; **strength-building** activities with weights to build muscles and bones; and **stretching and counter-strain** to make you more flexible and prevent injury to joints, ligaments and muscles.

To shed body fat, do cardiovascular and muscle-building exercises. Bigger muscles burn more body fat for energy, and an hour of cardiovascular exercise elevates your metabolic rate for up to 16 hours. To gain weight, build bigger muscles and stronger, denser bones with strength training. Cardiovascular exercise keeps you slim.

A fit body makes you more physically capable, looks sculpted, and makes you proud of your discipline, follow-through, effort and accomplishment. All these make you look and feel sexy. **Discipline and follow-through are sexy.**

Here's a trick to help your shape. In 30 minutes, you can eat more food than you need, and it takes 30 hours of exercise to burn off the excess. Be lazy. If you eat for only 20 minutes, you'll not have to do those 30 hours of exercise. You'll look and feel sexy if you stop eating before you're so full that your tummy hurts. Eat only till your hunger is gone. Eat only what you need and what is good for you.

Leave processed foods on the shelf. Buy fresh whole foods. Eat them raw as much as possible. Emphasize plant-based whole foods, and take a vitamin B12 supplement. Eat more vegetables than fruit. Eat raw, unsalted, unroasted, soaked seeds and nuts. They supply you with protein and energy-rich fats and oils. Use only oils made with health in mind and rich in undamaged omega-3 balanced with undamaged omega-6. Get them in glass bottles, boxed and refrigerated in stores. Stop using oils to cook, fry, deep-fry or stir-fry. Cook foods in water. Add good oils to foods on your plate when you're ready to eat them. **Throwing out your frying pan is sexy.**

Exercise for fun, and to build strength and sexy good shape. Do it because you can. Fall in love with making effort. **Making effort and being active is natural and sexy.**

Sunlight

Sunlight powers all cells, plants, animals and people on this planet. Sunlight provides almost all the energy that turns atoms into thousands of different molecules, which form the structure of the body of every creature. **Sunlight is sexy.**

Do you know that sunlight hangs out in bonds between atoms in molecules? When enzymes break down molecules, they free this stored sunlight to power the dance of chemical interactions in your cells to make other molecules. When you eat a so-called 'fuel' molecule (usually sugar/starch or fat/oil), life uses enzymes and oxygen to break down these fuels into water, carbon dioxide and energy. You pee out the water. You breathe out the carbon dioxide. The energy powers the work of your cells.

To complete this cycle, the sun's energy empowers plants to turn your water and carbon dioxide into sugar, starch, fat/oil and oxygen again.

Sunlight penetrates the human body, and can be converted into useable energy if we eat enough greens. However, most of the energy that fulfills our internal and external needs comes from sunlight held (or stored) in plant molecules, including those that are our fossil fuels. Hydroelectric power also comes from sunlight, which evaporates ocean water and raises it into colder, higher altitudes, where it turns into clouds. Rain falls, and we then harness the water's downhill flow back to the ocean.

In the process of photosynthesis, sunlight also energizes the production and release of free oxygen from its bondage in carbon dioxide and water, making that precious gas available for animals and us to breathe.

Gases in the atmosphere filter the sun's light. Mostly the visible wavelengths, which we and other organisms need, reach Earth's surface, along with some ultra-violet rays that can burn us. Remember, the sun is actually a huge nuclear furnace. Lucky for us, it's 93 million miles away. Its nuclear energy and radioactive rays can potentially destroy our delicate biological molecules and harm us.

What else does sunlight do for you? Sunlight creates the weather that brings clouds and rain over land to quench plants' thirst for it. Plants then grow and feed the animals as well. Sunlight and gravity create creeks, lakes and rivers. Sunlight creates each day for you to see. It hides behind the earth every night to let you sleep, rest and dream. Converted into heat on touching Earth, sunlight helps create wind, season and climate. In sunny places, you can harness sunlight directly for energy by means of solar cells. Falling on your skin, sunlight turns cholesterol into vitamin D. It also brings you a sense of general wellbeing. Lack of sunlight contributes to seasonal affective disorder. We truly are creatures of light.

Fresh Air

Fresh air is sexy. The freshness of fresh air is sexy. When you stand near a waterfall, you breathe in negative ions produced by water falling through the air. Although it is by nature colorless, tasteless and odorless, you can almost smell that fresh charged air. It fills your lungs with sexy energy and vitality.

Oxygen is your most precious element. All humans and most animals require it to keep body and soul together. A constant supply of oxygen that life extracts from air and pulls into your body allows your body to exist. A steady oxygen supply to your brain through blood in your carotid arteries allows you to externalize awareness. Block these arteries, and you will be unconscious in less than 3 seconds due to lack of oxygen. **Oxygen is sexy.**

Without breathing, permanent brain damage usually results after only 12 minutes. Cold temperature can slow down this damage. Oxygen is super-important.

You breathe in air with 20.95% oxygen, and you breathe out air with about 16% oxygen and about 5% carbon dioxide. CO_2, your breathing waste, is food for plants. In a 100-year lifetime at normal body weight and normal breathing, life draws 18 tons of free oxygen from the air into your body. That's 4+ times more than the total amount of all nutrients that life absorbs into your body from foods in that same lifetime.

Why is oxygen so sexy? Oxygen molecules react with other molecules to break down and release the bond-held sunlight energy in your body. That energy drives everything, from heartbeat and breath, to running marathons and molecular interactions. Sunlight powers most of the activities in your body's 10 trillion cells, 256 tissue types, and all your glands, organs and systems.

Where does sexy free oxygen, the most precious element in

the air that you breathe, come from? Living plants turn carbon dioxide plus water into sugar molecules. They string these together to make starches, cellulose and other kinds of plant fibers, the main constituents of tree trunks, shrubs, branches, stems and leaves. **Plants are sexy.** They release oxygen, your vital necessity. Plants don't need oxygen to live, but animals and humans can't live without it. Most of you know this half of the oxygen story.

The other half of the oxygen story is what happens when plants die. They rot. In this process of decomposition, as much oxygen as they made while alive reacts with the dead plants' cellulose and sugar molecules, and everything turns into carbon dioxide and water again. Did you learn this part in school? I did not. Why is it important? If plants, after dying, use up all the oxygen they made when they lived, it's a zero sum game. To have enough oxygen to breathe, you have to keep dead plants from rotting. Lucky for us, nature took care of it by burying a lot of them.

Here's something else you probably don't know. Living plants do NOT make all the free oxygen present in the air you breathe. They only make about ¼ of it. Where does the rest of the oxygen you need to breathe to live come from? That's where it gets seriously miraculous. ¾ of the oxygen in the air is from plants that died, that nature buried, and that therefore couldn't rot. They did not use up the oxygen they'd released while alive. Those buried green plants became fossil fuels: coal, oil and 'natural' gas, and all of the carbon-based chemicals we make from them: kerosene, gasoline, jet fuel, plastics and many others. You get to live because, buried, plants were separated from the oxygen they made, and left it in the air for you.

The fact that you breathe in air containing 21% oxygen and breathe out air with 16% oxygen points to the fact that you live on the top ¼ of the oxygen in earth's air. Presently living plants make only the bottom ¼ of it. Half of the oxygen in the air is left over from past plants, our present fossil fuels. Researchers studying this topic say that it took between 2.5 and 3.5 billion years for plants to live, make oxygen, die and get buried to raise oxygen in the air to present levels, to surround our planet with it, and to allow animals and us to exist.

Just over a century ago, industry began to dig up the dead buried plants–now fossil fuels–and burn them to produce the energy used by industry, air conditioning, motor vehicles, heavy machinery, and thousands of other energy sucking modern conveniences and gadgets. At present rates of fossil fuel use, they estimate that the oxygen in our air can go back down to 16% within only 300 to 15,000 years.

Is this cause for concern? Some experts estimate that human beings go into coma at about 19% oxygen, and at 16%, we absorb no oxygen and die. At 15% oxygen, a car won't start and fire won't burn. Burning fossil fuels is dangerous to our life. Solution: Keep fossil fuels buried and immediately replace them with safe, renewable non-carbon energy sources like solar, wind and water.

Fresh Water

Fresh water is sexy. Of all of your body's molecules, water is the most precious and important one. Animals require oxygen to exist, but ALL creatures must have water to live. Without water, no living creatures at all could survive. None. Zero. Zilch. Nada.

Water is a tiny molecule, but it constitutes 70% of your body weight, and 99% of all molecules in your body are water. Dehydration from lack of water makes you weak. Having no water to drink kills you within 7-8 days.

Most of the reactions that take place in your body actively involve water. For instance, when life breaks down molecules in your body, it splits a water molecule and adds a fragment of it to each broken end. When life reacts two molecules together, it subtracts a water fragment from the end of each molecule to make them sticky, so that they'll bond together.

In a lifetime of 100 years, life draws 88-110 tons of water into your body. By weight, that's 22-27 times more than the 4 tons of nutrients that life absorbs into your body in that time. Given that so much water courses through you, ensuring its purity and quality should be a high priority. You drink 12 times your body weight of water every year.

Sunlight evaporates ocean water, dumps it on land as rain and snow from which water flows, pulled down by gravity through rivers and lakes, back to the salty sea from which it came. In the process, water makes your planet both cool and green, and inhabits the plants and animals you eat. You drink this water. It bathes you internally, and quenches your thirst.

Fresh, cold and flowing water from a mountain stream below a glacier is sexy because it is healthy, and makes you feel vibrant. Milky white, oxygen- and mineral-rich, and micro-clustered, this water may even be alkaline. But fresh water does not stay fresh for long. By the time it is tap water in the city where you live, it is stale, old, dirty, and chlorine-poisoned. The good news is that specifically designed technology can make old, stale tap water fresh again.

Water is a highly interesting molecule. It breaks many of the usual rules of physical chemistry. For example, water is

- The only widely available molecule that exists in gas, liquid and solid states at normal planetary temperatures
- One of few molecules that expand when they freeze. That's why freezing water will break glass bottles and make a mess. It's also why ice freezes on top of water, leaving the water below liquid for fish to swim in
- Densest at 4°C, and at this temperature sinks to the bottom of a body of water. Water colder than 4°C will rise, and so will water warmer than 4°C
- The universal solvent, in which everything dissolves to some extent
- Able to form weak hydrogen bonds with other molecules, forming associations that change

molecular interactions. This may be one of the reasons why some people suggest that water has memory

- Able to hold an electric charge more effectively than other molecules

- Able to show a wide range of pH, from highly alkaline to highly acidic, with a wide range of practical properties, from detergent to antiseptic

In all, water shows more than 40 anomalies in its behavior. Many of these anomalies are theoretically super-complicated and beyond the scope of this book.

Globally, water is a widespread, abundant and effective sustainable natural source of clean industrial energy. Intelligent global water management can provide a great deal of sustainable local energy. It can end drought, dehydration and desertification. It can prevent crop failures and starvation, and prevent loss of soils by wind. Intelligent management of water can end flooding, erosion and wars over scarce water, land and food resources.

Fresh Food

Fresh whole raw organic food is sexy. Fresh, whole, raw, organically grown, toxin-free, in season, local, sun-ripe, mostly plant-based food is nature's health mandate for humans. Eat mostly that way to have the longest and healthiest physical existence.

Since the beginning, all creatures have eaten fresh and fermented whole, raw, organic foods in accordance with life's mandate. All except humans and the creatures we feed still eat their foods that way. Usurping nature's mandate, we create 'better living through chemistry', processing and cooking, and feed unnatural, 'toxified' junk foods to pets and other animals. Both they and we suffer health breakdowns as we replace living whole raw foods with less sexy options including cooked, fried and processed.

Do you eat fresh, whole, raw, organic foods that are sexy and healthy, or do you still eat processed and fried dead foods? Dead foods kill sexy by killing health. They dissipate your health and body prematurely. **Eating nutritious, raw, energizing, flavorful, fresh whole foods makes you sexy.**

Mostly plant-based

The research is now clear and convincing. Optimum health and longevity occur when you eat mostly plant-based whole foods and take a vitamin B12 supplement. It is that simple. Doing so, you also decrease your carbon footprint. Globally, the animals we raise for food require about six times more energy and water than plants, and burn up about five times more oxygen than all 8 billion people.

Processing removes and damages nutrients and may add toxins. It changes food quality from their sexy fresh, whole, raw, organic high-energy state to a low-energy unsexy, abused and dead state. Vote for health with your wallet. That's sexy. Care about what you put in your mouth. That's also sexy. The symphony of flavors, textures, colors and fragrances of plant-based whole foods is out-of-this-world sexy. **Eating nature in its living form is sexy.**

Greens, good oils and proteins

Where greens don't grow, people can't live. Much of the time, early hunters came home without meat. Then the family ate plants because they don't run away, don't fight back and are easy to hunt down and kill. Greens are your most important health-supporting foods.

Greens make almost everything you need. They store sunshine energy. You get both your internal food energy and your external heat and industrial energy from them. They dissolve and take up minerals from soil, and make them absorbable for you. They manufacture the essential vitamins, amino acids, proteins, fatty acids, fats and oils you need. Greens create the natural medicines in herbs and spices. They make protective antioxidants, phytonutrients and gene-modulators for you. They hold water in the soil and moderate weather and climate. Raw plants supply protective probiotic bacteria and provide fibers (prebiotics) that are food for probiotics. The enzymes they contain help your digestion. Plants also make the oxygen you breathe. Plants make materials for your clothing and shelter. They need you for nothing. You need them for everything. **Respect, revere and eat the plants that make you sexy.**

Eat good oils. **Good oils are sexy.** They provide stable, performance raising, extended energy. They calm your craving and addiction to mood flipping, insulin-spiking, life-shortening un-sexy refined sugars and starches. They beautify your skin, raise your thinking capacity, and keep your cells, organs and systems healthy and sexy.

Avoid heat-damaged and fried oils, as well as frying and fried foods like the plague. All oils rob you of your sexy. They lower your energy level, inflame you and raise your risk of cancer. Inflamed, you have more pain, and you'll more likely support thieves of sexy: diabetes, dementia, heart disease, cancer, osteoporosis, arthritis. **Not frying is sexy.**

Eat fresh whole, mostly plant-based foods including fresh, unroasted, unsalted seeds and nuts. You'll never be short of protein unless you're a bodybuilder taking steroids. A cow makes steaks and milk out of grass. Horses, elephants, rabbits and gorillas are made entirely out of grass and leaves, plus water and oxygen. The occasional worm or insect on their plant-based foods makes them not perfectly vegan, but close. The idea that you have to eat eggs, meat, dairy or fish to get enough protein is largely based on the ads of the industries that sell you these products.

In India, 300 million Hindus belong to the Brahmin caste. Obligate vegetarians, they eat a tablespoon of soured milk with each meal, to get probiotics and vitamin B12. They eat no flesh. Fish, fowl, red meat and eggs are off the menu. Whole plant-based foods have enough protein for Brahmin requirements (the warrior caste does eat flesh).

Limit fruits, lower carbs. Carbohydrate-rich foods like potatoes, grains and corn, and the baked 'goods', pasta, fried foods and chips made from them, as well as desserts, soft drinks and sweets are unnatural and not sexy. They cause swings in your insulin, blood sugar and mood, and make you addicted, overweight, obese, diabetic, heart-diseased and short-lived.

Beans, lentils, and chickpeas can be good food for some people. Some fruit is good, but nature consists of much more greens than fruit. Ratio? In nature, the ratio of greens to fruit is 10+: 1. In my experience, that's a healthy ratio of greens to fruit for humans.

Essential nutrients

18 minerals, 13 vitamins, 8 amino acids and 2 fatty acids are 'essential' by a specific definition developed by researchers. Essential nutrients are those that fit the following definition.

- Life can't make them from anything else in your body, but you must have them to live and be healthy, and so you must get them from foods or supplements
- Insufficient intake (getting too little) impairs your health; you get deficiency symptoms that are degenerative in nature, get worse with time, and kill you if you don't get enough long enough
- They reverse all problems that come from not getting enough if, before death, you return enough to a diet that contains too little of them (by definition, death is not reversible)

- Life knows exactly how to use them to make a healthy body, provided you take responsibility for making sure that enough of each lands in your body for life to do its job

Most essential nutrients come from a program of organic, whole, plant-based foods, herbs and spices. You can augment this program with supplements. Don't make the silly mistake of thinking you can eat junk and fix it by popping supplement pills.

Antioxidants, Phytonutrients, Gene modulators

These come from foods, herbs and spices but some are also available as supplements. Food first! A supplement may be useful in addition, but not instead of foods.

Fuel

You need a source of energy. In order of best to worst fuels: Good oils > good fats > unrefined carbs > protein > refined starch > sugar. Good oils are the best fuel and also contain two sexy essential fatty acids that optimize your health. Small amounts of unrefined carbs (brown rice, quinoa, whole oats, yams) can be good for health, but do not overeat them, because you'll gain weight and get a long list of unsexy problems if you eat more than your body burns. How do you know? A pinch test on your belly or your butt should come up empty. If it doesn't, lower your carb intake.

Digestion

Digestion takes place outside your body. This may sound strange, but the inside of your digestive tract is not inside your body. It is a tube through your middle and the foods you eat are digested in that tube outside your body. There, enzymes break down foods and life pulls into your body (absorbs) only the nutrients it needs to build and re-build your body. Any material that's not useful is not absorbed. It passes down and out as waste. Probiotics, digestive enzymes and prebiotic fiber aren't essential nutrients but they're essential for health. Let us take a look at what each one does.

1. **Probiotics are highly sexy friendly bacteria** that protect you from viruses, yeasts, fungi and bacteria that could make you sick. They also protect you from 'rot' bacteria whose job it is to recycle your body after you die, but not while you're alive. Probiotics protect the delicate inside lining of your gut. They make some vitamins. They make short chain fatty acids that protect your colon. They keep your digestive tract, as well as your liver, brain, immune system, weight, and cardiovascular system normal. They also protect your skin and all your body openings from infections by unfriendly microbes.

   In nature, probiotics cover raw foods and inhabit the layer of fermenting plant materials on top of soils. They also live in the breast ducts and birth canal of mammals, including humans. The sexiest and most powerful 'indigenous' or human-adapted probiotics exist naturally in your digestive tract. They survive strong bile and stomach acid and implant in the lining of your gut. There they live and help health for about 10 days. Dairy-based 'transient' probiotics live only a day in your digestive tract before they exit your body.

   When you cook foods, you kill the sexy probiotics that you need. Replace them with human-adapted, carefully designed age- and condition-specific probiotic blends.

2.   **Digestive enzymes** **are** **sexy** **proteins** that break down foods in your digestive tract to free the nutrient building blocks. If you eat sexy raw foods, the enzymes they contain help to digest these foods. Your body also makes different kinds of digestive enzymes in your digestive tract. These ensure complete digestion and optimum absorption of the nutrients. When you cook foods, you destroy the enzymes present in raw foods. For sexy health, replace the lost enzymes with a supplement of different enzymes with each meal to completely break down the proteins, fats and starches you eat. Good digestion is sexy. Gut pain, bloating and gas are not.

3.   **Sexy prebiotic fibers come from plants.** They're the preferred food for the friendly probiotics that play health-protective roles in your body. All plant-based whole foods provide prebiotic fiber that makes you healthier and sexier. Animal-based foods contain none.

Poisons

What is poison, and why is poison poisonous? Poison is any substance (or energy) that blocks, inhibits or derails natural interactions between the molecules that build and run the biochemical architecture of your body. They are poisonous because they interfere with natural interactions between molecules in your cells. Avoid poisons. Use natural ways to detoxify. Breathe deep, drink lots of fresh water, eat fresh, whole, organic, plant-based foods that contain prebiotic fibers, and support your liver in its detoxification functions with herbs and spices. And sweat. It's one of the most effective and underused ways to detoxify.

The longer a poison stays in your body, the longer it messes with optimum sexy health. It's well known that you can sweat out water-soluble toxins quite easily, and they'll show up in the water part of your sweat. It's less well known that oil-soluble toxins tend to be more toxic than water-soluble ones. Fats in your cells and tissues store them. They're more difficult to remove than water-soluble toxins. The good news: You can sweat out oil-soluble toxins by increasing your intake of good oils made with health in mind.

Use enough good oils made with health rather than shelf life in mind to make your skin soft and smooth. That'd be about one tablespoon of oil per 50 pounds (25kg) of body weight per day, and more if your skin still feels dry. You need more good oil in winter than in summer. To sweat out oil-soluble toxins, take up to twice more oil. Oil-soluble poisons like pesticides, PCBs, dioxins, Agent Orange, benzene, toluene and others rob you of your energy. Sweat 15-30 minutes every day. Sauna is an easy way. Do it for 3-6 months. Use good oil to drive oil-soluble toxins out of your body through your skin. You can measure the toxins in the oil part of your sweat, and you can monitor their decrease in your body. Have a health care professional supervise it.

I did this and experienced the benefit of good oils after pesticide poisoning in the 1980s. Lasseter's group in the US detoxified Vietnam veterans poisoned by Agent Orange. Sweating is the best way to detoxify. It prevents poisons from damaging your liver and kidneys. In sweating out oil-soluble toxins, your worst symptom might be a temporary skin rash. As poisons leave your body, your energy, your sexy and your health improve.

Frying is the single worst action human invention ever developed regarding foods and health. Fried foods fry your health and your sexiness. Throw out your frying pan. **NOT frying is sexy**. It's the biggest single contribution you can make to physical sexy. To cook, use water. Add good undamaged oils made with health in mind to foods after they come off the heat. Replace the minerals, probiotics, enzymes, amino acids and vitamins that water-cooking leaches, loses, kills, damages or destroys.

Excess carb consumption is the main reason for epidemic overweight and obesity. In 1979, experts recommended that we eat more carbs. In 20 years, overweight rose from 25 to 65% of the population. Consuming more carbs from grains, corn, potatoes and other sweet and starchy foods (bread, pasta, chips, snacks, soft drinks, sweets and desserts) messed up sexy, big-time. When you eat carbs you burn them or you wear them. It's the body's law that excess unburned carbs turn into fats in your body. To improve body functions and physical health, lower your intake of carbs.

The weight (fat) you gain from eating too many carbs sows the seeds for many future problems: cravings, gorging and purging, as well as overeating and obesity. These go on to diabetes, cardiovascular disease and cancer. Excess weight destroys your body and shortens your time on earth.

The weight you gain from water retention due to inflammation from ingesting pesticides, plastics, industrial chemicals and fried foods, or from lack of probiotics in your gut starts many different problems.

Clear skin, good posture and relaxed alertness are sexy. When you live present in your body and are not 'lost in thought', you're at home in yourself, and that's sexy. Intense physical activity that breaks a sweat carries toxins from your body out through your skin. If you don't sweat, these toxins can remain in your skin, making your skin pale instead of radiant, and enhance the risk of zits, skin infections and other less sexy conditions.

The good posture that results when you tone your body through physical activity is sexy. Weak muscle tone encourages you to slouch. Conscious of your body, you are, feel and appear sexy to others. Moving deliberately, you feel and look sexy. When you practice being comfortably present in your body, you practice being sexy.

5

MENTAL HEALTH 2:
Survival Smarts

Survival

SURVIVAL SMARTS IS THE FIFTH key part of total sexy health designed by nature. You contend daily with survival issues that take place between your body and a friendly or unfriendly outside world. Survival issues include protection, safety, clothing and shelter. They also include reproduction, parenting, education and fulfilling basic needs.

Safety and reproduction are the key survival needs. One makes sure that the race goes on. The other protects and cares for your children. Deliberate, inspired creation of safety is sexy, and serves both of these needs. Survival smarts are part courage and part skill. Courage is *showing up* with presence and power, ready to engage. Skillful methods and procedures determine *how to act* into an emerging situation.

Our distant ancestors' stress was mainly about dealing with physical dangers in order to ensure physical survival. Today, most stress is mental. But your brain, body, immune and hormonal systems respond to mental and physical stress in the same way. While your mind, made up of thoughts, concepts, beliefs, memories and imagination is not actually real, you use it to set direction and limits for your actions—what you will and will not do. These determine limitations, direction, goals and destinies. The mental part of survival pain is usually called stress. There's too much to do. Fear of failure and living under pressure call your survival into question.

You're surrounded by gifts and dangers. You use gifts to make physical existence safer, easier or more bearable. You avoid dangers by fighting, fleeing, freezing or withdrawing. Facing or anticipating dangers, life creates stress molecules that prime your body to flee or fight.

The physical activities involved in dealing with stress break down the stress molecules. If these are not broken down, stress molecules linger and negatively affect your health. This is especially likely to happen in mentally stressful situations in which you lack options to act physically. Inactive, you stew in chronic stress chemistry that damages health.

Today, most of your chronic stressors are like that—mental. You're under job pressure to perform to specifications in bosses' minds and you may not know exactly what the boss expects of you. That's stressful. You may have competition that puts pressure on you. People may scheme to get your position at work by undermining you. Your boss may be unfair but you don't get to beat him up. Your co-workers may criticize, belittle or even abuse you, but you can't quit the job. You may be subject to indecent proposals and worry about losing the job if you reject improper advances. All these can lead you to stressful fear, anger and anxiety. These kinds of chronic stress burn out your adrenal glands and can be destructive to all of your body systems. We'll talk later in this chapter about the anatomy of stress and its cure. It's simpler than you may think.

Survival requires your attention, but ultimately your body will fail. If survival is your only purpose for living, your later years will be filled with anxiety and fear as you watch your body age, wrinkle, slow down and deteriorate. Making survival your reason for living is not sexy, so create a larger purpose to live for, and give your energy, mind and body to that. It can keep you charged and vibrant (which is sexy) until the day your body wears out. Live aware that you are life, rather than your body. You are the body's owner. In the end, leave your worn out body without fear or regret, knowing that you lit up the world.

We'll consider the process of dying in Chapter 12. It's an enlightening topic. While the experience of death is not externally sexy, it is internally profound. We'll leave that conversation till we get through a few other chapters that set the stage for it.

Processing Change

Change triggers your survival mechanisms for both attraction and protection. How does it work? To determine whether a situation is danger or opportunity requires you to check it out. When nothing in your environment changes because there's nothing going on, you need neither to assess nor to take action. Everything is fine. But the moment that something changes, you have to identify the change and respond or react. The way life made you is marvelously interesting, in that change in your surroundings draws your awareness outward through your senses to focus on the change. You see something move, its color or shape change, hear it, feel it, smell it or even taste it.

You assess the change. It may turn out to be nothing out of the ordinary (boring), in which case you relax and forget about it. It might be attractive (love), in which case you take notice, perhaps smile and find a way to move closer to it. It could be dangerous (threat), in which case you shift into 'fight or flight' mode. All of it happens automatically, mostly on a subconscious 'autonomic' level below your normal awareness. But there's a foundation to your reaction and our task here is to become aware of and examine that foundation.

Let me say it another way. Life directs your awareness out through your senses to any change in your environment. It's important for survival to rapidly find out whether the change is friendly or unfriendly. You ignore it if it's not important to survival, approach it if it enhances survival and go into protective mode if it endangers survival. You use anger to fight it if you deem it's weaker than you, and flee if you fear that it's stronger.

You don't need this mechanism in the womb, where it is safe and all your needs are met without any effort on your part. The moment you're born, however, you need to learn about the world in which your body will live and survive, using the process of noticing and attending to change in your environment. The way you process change begins to develop soon after birth.

In nature, this survival mechanism proved to be good for enhancing the chance of, well, surviving. Human beings however, have also invented many ways to take advantage of others by targeting this basic survival mechanism. Knowing that change draws your attention, I can move your focus wherever I want by deliberately creating changes. It works every time. To get your attention, I change sounds, colors and movements.

Most of us are not aware or disciplined enough to ignore the changes around us, even though today, virtually none of them threaten our survival. It's why harmless TV images that consist of moving pictures and changing sounds are so addictively attractive. They pull us in by our built-in biological survival mechanism.

To keep your attention, those who produce shows put changes in front of your range of senses, or get your attention with powerful emotions like uncertainty, love and fear. Sellers and marketers do it, too. So do autocrats in government and religion, who sometimes make laws just to keep you on edge, and use threats of jail or hellfire to control your attention and behavior.

Some create crisis after crisis and spin after spin to keep you busy with them. They use fear, love and confusion, your most basic survival response triggers, as tools to attract and direct your sensory awareness to what they want you to think and do.

Effective con artists and manipulators know how to use such methods to get you to think, say and do almost anything.

Skilled attention seekers know how to keep us busy with them. Be the news. Be outrageous. Be controversial. Contradict yourself. Confuse them. Create variety. Make faces. Threaten them. Use words that trigger survival responses. Inspire fear and anger with pictures of pain, loss and destruction. Embrace. Paint pretty, changing images. Associate fads with sexy energy and enthusiasm. Tell them you love them. Say that you will save them. Hire sexy people to embody and promote the facade. If you don't do it, people create their own sexy situations and forget you; then you lose power over them. You know that it works and how it does. Every day it works on you, and every day you work it on others.

Try this exercise: For one day, notice the ways in which individuals and social groups use change to focus your attention on what they want to get from or unload on you. Have fun with it. See if and how you can stop being distracted by changes designed to pull you out to what they want you to notice, away from the sexy wonder of your own life. For bonus points, watch yourself doing the same thing to others.

Emergencies

No matter how well you plan your days, projects, journeys, company trajectories and sexy life, something unexpected always happens. An unforeseen emergency emerges. You don't see it coming, so you're not prepared, and it can easily become dangerous or deadly. You go into stress mode to avoid or prevent harm, seek protection or find safety. You plan ahead to anticipate ways in which things can go wrong. You minimize crises, but crises still happen.

"The best-laid plans of mice and men gang aft agley (go often awry)", said the Scottish poet Robbie Burns. The Boy Scouts' motto is, "Be prepared", even though emergencies can't be 100% anticipated, and not all disasters can be prevented. That's why you take courses to learn the skills you need to manage crises during crisis-free times. The worst time to take such a course is during the emergency. When the ship hits the fan, you want to already know what options for action you have, and be as ready as you can possibly be.

What's the best preparation for emergencies? Develop helpful skills. Preparedness is sexy. That's why we learn martial arts and other skills of self-defense, for instance. That's why soldiers, sailors, pilots and first responders develop and practice life-saving skills in artificially created, simulated situations. The mistakes they make can be used to learn and improve without producing irreversible damage or fatalities. Lucky for us!!

What's not nearly as well taught as these skills is courage and audacity that may be even more important in the face of emergencies. How do you keep calm in the midst of the storm? It's easy enough to declare, 'I AM the storm!!' It's much harder to actually pull that off. How do you stay alert and present in the midst of a crisis? It's tough until you get good at being present in your calm, cool, collected and powerfully sexy internal presence. That takes committed practice. Fully present, you most effectively respond to crises. How do you access that internal state? It's a good question. Hit with crisis, some folks become anxious, fearful, confused and disoriented. Paralyzed, they don't respond well. More trauma and increased casualties result.

To learn the sexy calmness, begin by knowing that something within you is always awake and aware. It cannot be disturbed or made fearful, and is always calm because it is formless, not mental, indestructible and always filled with calm courage. Learn and practice focusing there. When you keep your focus on awareness and life, you greatly enhance your chance of remaining stable and fully functional in the midst of danger and chaos.

When your awareness goes only to your body, which can be hurt or destroyed, you feel fear, and might run to save yourself when your purpose is to help others. 'Heroes' are sexy. They stay strong and focused on their purpose in the midst of danger and crisis. They risk death to bring others out of danger. That's super-sexy. Sometimes they perish in the process. Then you celebrate their heroism at the funeral. That's awesomely sexy.

If you anticipate and foresee the potential for danger, you can create and put in place safety procedures that protect or save you without sacrifice. Such wisdom could be more widely applied than it is. For instance, in places known for earthquakes and tidal waves, it's unwise to erect buildings close to the shore. In Japan, they knew it wasn't a matter of whether there'd be earthquake and tidal wave, but merely a matter of when.

You wouldn't build a nuclear plant on that shore, knowing its breakdown would cause widespread environmental contamination with radioactive poisons that last for centuries, end up in your food supply and seriously impact health. You'd not set sloppy building specs as they did in Chernobyl. You wouldn't use cheap building materials to pocket more profit. Life is the sexy treasure. Everything else, including money, is meant to protect, serve and care for life.

Life Killing Stress

Stress is the great global disease of modern times and the root of much of what ails us. I'm in a hurry. You're in a hurry. Everybody is chasing around, cutting corners, trying to get stuff done. Human beings turn into human doings. You remain oblivious of the deepest, sexiest part of your being in which there is never and can never be any stress. Stress cannot reach there. That depth of your being is deeper than stress can dive.

Change, you know, attracts your awareness outward, away from your sexy being, to assess and respond with a view to survival. In non-emergency states, your awareness could be in touch with your sexy being. But, the way you habitually operate, it's most likely to be following thoughts of crisis even in the absence of crisis, or engaged in fantasies and distractions. You're good at bringing our awareness outward from within but have little training in or practice of moving your awareness inward from outside.

How does stress work? Can you get a handle on it? Can you live without stress in the midst of stress? Once you know how it works and observe it working within you, it's not difficult. Here's how it goes.

Let's say you're at rest and your awareness is in touch with life inside the core of your sexy being. Most people are in THAT place only during deep sleep, but then unaware of it. And so, in our experience, this feeling of being in touch with life does not exist. We miss it. It's there but it's not there for us. That's the nature of experience. It's real when you're in it, and it doesn't exist for you when you're not in it.

For a moment, just pretend. There you are all quiet, calm and sexy within yourself. A change happens. Immediately, your awareness disconnects from your quiet sexy calm and moves outward to the source of the change. The change that attracts your attention is always about a person or a situation; someone or something. You identify a threat to survival. You react/respond with 'fight or flight'. In your mind, you think, "That person or situation stressed me." But is that really true? It is not. Let me explain.

People have different perceptions of what is stressful and what is not. Stressed out of my mind by an event, I could stand beside someone who remains utterly unstressed by the same event. What's the difference between us? My emotional reaction to that person or event gets me into a flap. The other person is unaffected because it has no emotional meaning for her or him.

So I have a question for you? If I, like the other person, didn't give a hoot about the event, would I get stressed? You know the answer. A person or event about which I'm neutral does not stress me. The truth is that it's not the event that stresses me; it's what I think in my head regarding the event. This means that I use the event as a trigger (or an excuse) to stress myself. Think about it. I blame a person or event for thoughts I create in my own mind. Is this also true for you? I think you know it is.

Remaining neutral, you will not be stressed. It takes effort to become aware of what you bring to people and events that turns on your stress response. You may think someone SHOULD act or something SHOULD be a certain way, but the person or situation is not how you made up in your mind it should be. You get stressed when you want people and events to be different from the way they are, and don't accept people and events as they are. That's the basic recipe for stress. Accept people and events as they are, and you own the sexy equanimity that goes with acceptance. **Acceptance is sexy.**

So what can you do about it? Would you like to hear my cheeky short answer? I'll follow it with an explanation. My cheeky answer is that you should mind your own business!!! You learned to think that you have to have an opinion on everything in the world. But you don't. You have another option, which is to follow your rules for how you live, and to accept that others live by other rules. As long as they don't impose their opinion on you, you don't have to impose yours on them. Acceptance is more powerful and sexy than judgment, and it works better in your life.

I said you should mind your own business. What's your business? I'll tell you, even though it is not my business to tell what your business should be. In the broadest, deepest, most profound sense, your business is to be, feel and enjoy the awesome, wondrous, magnificent, divinely sexy gift of your life by being fully present in its grandeur. That's extremely sexy.

You were given life as a gift to enjoy. Enjoying it is not selfish. **Enjoying life is sexy.** If you don't enjoy it, it's a wasted gift because no one else can enjoy it for you. Enjoying your existence is your business. Let me ask you one more question. If you're busy enjoying your own sexy life and have no time to mind everyone else's, do you get stressed? No. You don't have time to trigger yourself by making judgments.

Many of you think you need stress to motivate you to do what needs to be done. It's not true. Usually, stress makes you less effective. You don't have to feel stressed to do what needs to be done. Children get more done playing than 'grownups' do working. Why? Playing children are unstressed, so they're free to create. They invent games, act them out and learn a lot. Content adults tend to do more than stressed adults. You do better work when you focus and enjoy what's before you than when your mind is generating anxiety, anger and mean thoughts.

Feeling calm, accepting and content from the personal roots within you cures stress. These feelings are always in you. Bring and keep your awareness there while you attend to your tasks in the world. In time and with practice, you learn to be present and aware in both your own sexy inner being and the external world at the same time. Some call it 'simultaneous presence'. **Simultaneous presence is sexy**. In that state, there's no stress. It takes time to get good at it. Some situations may continue for a while to trigger stress within you. With practice, you'll let these triggers go because nothing feels better with stress than it does without it.

Don't' Burn Out

Suppose that you choose not to practice getting present to your own magnificence. You continue to let the world come at you fast. You continue not to have your essential calm presence meet and stand up to the world. When you are not present in your sexy inner power, some of what comes at you will bowl you over and overwhelm you. Have you heard this saying of Alexander Hamilton? 'If you don't stand for something, you'll fall for anything.'

Not present to your life and power, the world knocks you over. You feel surprised, abused and misused. You lose health, become depressed and develop resentment that fries your adrenals. You may create a victim personality, complain, and eventually burn out. It's not sexy! Chronic stress leads to burnout and exhaustion that can cause serious physical degeneration and bring early death.

No discussion about stress carries on for long before the name

Hans Selye comes up. Who's he? Selye studied stress and came up with a theory of stress in the late 1930s. He spent the next 40 years expanding on the topic. He observed and described the way creatures deal with stress as a 3-stage process that he called the 'General Adaptation Syndrome' (GAS).

He called the first stage **alarm**. You react to threats to your wellbeing. Perception and interpretation lead to a mobilization of fight or flight response, which involves adrenal glands (cortisol & adrenaline), the hypothalamus in the brain, the sympathetic nervous system and the master pituitary gland below the brain.

The second stage he called **resistance**. You remain on high alert against the continuing stressor, and heart rate, blood pressure, blood sugar and breathing remain elevated, but other than that, everything appears normal. Your system continues to direct effort against the source of stress.

He called the third state **exhaustion**. Over time, a sustained stressor burns you out. All your stress-fighting resources get used up. At this point, a small additional stress can make you sick or kill you. GAS can be body-wide or local, and involves inflamed tissues and the immune system's repair processes. Selye's work outlined what happens in a body that is the victim of stress.

Selye did NOT address the fact that something within you is beyond stress and can never get stressed or burned out. When you dwell there, you leave the stress outside. **Leaving stress outside is sexy**. Of course, if the stress physically threatens you, running (if you assess you'll lose) or fighting (if you assess you'll win) is important for survival. But most of your stressors today are mental. In actuality, they're not life threatening but you perceive them to be so and the same system kicks into gear.

Most people don't distinguish clearly between the physical and mental stresses with which they deal in their day. Bring your sexy awareness back to life. This removes you from the mental stress realm. When you do that, you become more resilient and deal more productively with mental stresses. Instead of merely coping with stress, you shift your focus to appreciating and enjoying your life. **Appreciation is sexy.**

Ultimately, the only cure for most of the stresses in your life is the sexy feeling of inner peace, contentment and calmness. No stress can reach that place within you. Not even death can go there. From that place, you see what's not apparent when your amygdala has been hijacked. From that place, choices and options in meaning and action abound and are available to you. These lead to better outcomes and an improved quality of your sexy life.

I've had thousands of conversations with people who felt stressed, overwhelmed and burned out. I tell them, "I'll walk with you into your deepest darkness, and we'll walk out together back into the sexy light." I don't fear darkness because I know that I'm the light in my darkness, as you are the light in yours. You can know that light because you ARE that light. **Being light is sexy.**

Did you know? The sexy light in you has never met the unsexy darkness in you. Where there's light, there's no darkness. Where there's darkness, there's no light. Light and darkness don't coexist and they can't talk to each other. Furthermore, darkness yields to light but light does not yield to darkness. Why is that? Light is a presence of power and energy. Darkness is absence of the power and energy of light. Darkness is nothing. No matter what's going on, you can choose to give attention to the power and presence of light or the nothing and absence of darkness.

Safety

1. As <u>body</u>, you fight, flee, freeze or withdraw
2. As <u>survival mind</u>, you assess change and then decide on actions for the body to take to optimize your chance of survival
3. As <u>creative mind</u>, you design strategies for safety that minimize crises

4. As <u>life</u>, you are the ever-indestructible feeling of safety

When you find your safety within your own being, you can more easily create safety on the outside also. You build a stronger, safer house. Sexy. You build your house above the reach of tidal waves. Sexy. You communicate from feeling safe to create a more harmonious relationship. Sexy. You don't play with fire, even though you can. It's sexy to live in the wisdom of knowing that just because you CAN do something doesn't mean that you MUST do it.

Even though we CAN dig up more of them, it's best to leave fossil fuels in the ground and develop energy sources with fewer detrimental side effects. Even though we know how to use nuclear weapons, we're wiser and safer not using them. Even though we can continue to, we no longer need to test them. We know they work. Just because we have enough money to start a war does not mean we should start a war. Just because we can patent poisons and make obscene profits on their sale does not mean we should ignore health and restrict medical practice to dispensing these poisons.

Just because your government keeps you in crises does not mean you should commit your life to them, when you could just as easily live in peace. Just because you can go into debt doesn't mean you should go into debt. You can live more disciplined than that. Just because religious and political leaders foment hate against other groups does not mean that you should listen to them, or hate your neighbor and those who follow other ways of thinking.

Live with your awareness in touch with contentment, the place of peace and safety within you. This protects you from an undisciplined mind. **Peace and safety are sexy**. Your awareness focused in peace frees your inspiration, which becomes your source of innovation. Using it, build the safety that minimizes crisis, and spend more of your time enjoying your life.

You need less energy to enjoy full presence than to neglect

it, to abuse your self, and to deal with the outfall. **Full presence is sexy**. You need less energy to live in harmony with your neighbor than you do to live in conflict with him or her. It takes less effort to build a solid house than it does to build one that falls apart and constantly needs repair.

It's easier to build a peaceful world where citizens respect themselves and help each other than to build a world in conflict, at war and in rubble requiring reconstruction. It's easier to embody the highest common denominators of peace, truth and love than it is to live any other way.

Stay present in the sexy majesty of life within you. For that, you need no outside help. You only have to be with yourself. From that sexy feeling, everything else flows more naturally without much struggle.

In that feeling, you can most effectively use your energy for the good of all at the expense of none. You can think 'us all, inclusive,' globally. You protect, care for and enjoy life, body, others and planet. Be in that sexy feeling. Without it, nothing works so well. **Grounded and practical is sexy**.

Life created your sexy brain and mind to serve as its computer. It has several functions:

1. Collect information from within the body

2. Gather information through the senses from the external environment

3. Interpret the meaning of inputs regarding both aspects of physical survival: protection and procreation

4. Choose the best plans for action based on input and interpretation

5. Act on these plans

6. Assess the results, learn from them and modify accordingly

Used in this way, brain and mind are sane and sexy.

Life has a clear purpose for its computer. Regarding mental health, think of this purpose as the foundation of sexy sanity: Deliberate, generous forward global thinking directed to enable all humanity to benefit. **Sanity is sexy.**

Sanity results when life informs its computer with the experience of self-knowledge. **Self-knowledge is sexy.** When your awareness disconnects from your life, life's computer loses its director. Then, like the sorcerer's apprentice, it can make a mess of everything and be unable to clean up that mess. Disconnected from life, the computer can give highly destructive reactive commands.

My most comprehensive definition of insanity is a mind out of touch with the heart, or your life's computer out of touch with your life. When you live out of touch with life, reactions to external input, arbitrary ideas, memories and imagination run your world.

Each problem on the planet begins with disconnection from the heart. Each problem on the planet improves with re-connection to the heart. Feel the sexy life you are in the heart of your being. **Heart-felt is sexy.**

6

SOCIAL HEALTH:
Social Ease, Connection

Membership

SOCIAL EASE AND CONNECTION IS the sixth key part of total sexy health designed by nature. A few years ago, a credit card company ad trumpeted, 'Membership has its privileges.' It's true, and membership also has limitations, disadvantages and restrictions. What's the difference? I'm not strong on blind faith. I want to know.

My parents were children in Europe during in the first world war and the communist revolution that followed, then lived through the 'great' depression, and then managed to also survive the second world war. After all of that, they were intensely happy to leave Europe. They questioned a lot. "Not everything you hear or read is true," they said. An ardent student, I learned from them to be skeptical, and to examine if what people say or write is actually true. **Being a skeptic is sexy**. Proudly question what you hear and read!!! When something is not true but you believe it to be true, it'll cause you problems. Some say that every problem in the world begins with a lie. What do you think? I could make a strong case for it.

Lies rob you of choice. They're a form of dictatorship. Unsexy. Knowing truth makes you free. You can choose. **Freedom is sexy.** The choices you make based on wrong 'facts' enslave you. How do you know whether something is true?

Ask, "What's the standard? True to what? In what context? Compared to what?" For Earthlings, the key answers come down to life's standards. What is true to life? **True to life is sexy.**

Why true to life? Something can be true to culture, fad, work, paranoid fantasy or whim but not be true to life. Life is the standard here because it makes this fragile planet unique, precious and sexy. Life (not money, ideas, or things) is Earth's greatest treasure and currency. Not only is life is your true wealth (without it, you are nothing and have nothing), but life is also your wisdom, power and magnificence.

THAT's why life is the standard. When your thoughts, words or actions don't protect, serve and care for life, hold those thoughts and refrain from acting on them because they aren't true to life. Much of what you hear and read isn't true to life but serves other, less noble agendas.

Social health involves membership in groups larger than your individual self. On the negative side, groups enable you to let others lead you. They can give you a sense of belonging before you've discovered that by nature, you first and foremost belong to life. In groups you can find a place to hide, another 'mother' to take care of you and a place where you can duck out and let others do the heavy lifting. Before you join any groups, come to terms with some basic aspects of yourself, such as

- Accepting self-responsibility
- Being in-dependent on life
- Standing on your own feet
- Talking straight and walking tall

- Making your own decisions regarding how to live true to life
- Knowing what to do with your time on Earth
- Being clear what you bring that contributes to the group

The positive, sexy side to external belonging begins after you've taken charge of your sexy self by being fully present in it. **Full presence is sexy.** Once you know that life takes perfect care of you and you are whole, there's nothing better and more fun than pitching in and helping others improve the quality of their lives. You're sexy when you do that.

Then, within the rules of the group and the roles you accept, based on your individual gifts and talents, you can laugh and play, connect and communicate, put your shoulder to the common wheel, protect members and bring greater thriving to all. **Thriving is sexy.** Contributing to the thriving of others is super-sexy.

Belonging is a two-edged sword. If you're not whole, you shame your community, add extra burdens to the members and contribute to the destruction of the group. If you are whole, you influence others in the direction of their sexy wholeness, bring wisdom and light, and contribute to the sexy, life-based radiance of your fellow members.

The key is YOUR state of being. In what state of being do you live? In what state of being do you want to live? Practice it. Be that. Hold to it. Be present. Be real. Be lit up from within by the sexy light of life that you are. Help where you can. Make it work for all. Give your unique talent freely.

Imagine social groups where all members live that way. Imagine the world with 8 billion citizens all committed to living that way, sexy beyond race, gender, religion and nation; feeling whole, fulfilled and present in life. Do you want to be the kind of person who adds that kind of value to the social groups to which you belong? I surely want to be that kind of a person and to work to create that kind of a social group and world.

Acceptance

Imagine a social group in which the members unconditionally accept and celebrate the talent, uniqueness and contribution of each individual. Is that even possible? It is, and it's super-helpful in a world in which you live surrounded by strongly held and unfounded opinions. But it begins with self-acceptance. It's a challenge. **Self-acceptance is sexy.**

You don't fully accept yourself. All your life, you've been told you should be different from the way you are. It began with others around you telling you that you're not enough. You bought into it and now, with no provocation, you take yourself down daily, repeating to yourself sub-consciously that you're not enough and not worthy of love, and have to keep trying to become better. But if you begin with the conviction that you're not enough, nothing you do can fix that. You have to drop the conviction.

Where is the biological, real evidence and proof that you're not enough? Did life ever tell you that? No, life never said that. When life decides you're a failure, it unceremoniously recycles your body. The fact that you're alive, human and here is PROOF that you're enough and life wants you here. Stop your *sexy-choking self-BS.*

Take a deep, sexy breath. **Breathing is sexy.** Let go of your thoughts and feel inward. **Feeling inward is sexy.** Close your eyes and look inward. Listen into your being. Ooh, you are so beautifully rich and full in complete stillness. Do you feel it? Do you hear it? Can you see it? Do this every day. How else will you learn to get and stay out of the 'not enough' program in your head? How else will you discover that you've always been loved and cared for, and have always been sexy? Nothing's ever been wrong with what you, in essence, are.

Only in thinking disconnected from life can you invent

self-rejection. Reject that kind of thinking instead of rejecting yourself. Nothing you think is ever true. All thoughts are made up, unreal, created out of nothing and arbitrarily conjured into being. Yet you desperately cling to them like they were gospel truths. **Stepping out of your thoughts is sexy.**

Let them go, and replace them with the sexy feeling of self-presence and from THAT experience, re-think, re-write, re-work and re-define who you are. **Self-presence is sexy.** Accept your whole being. You are life. You are sexy. You're not

- What you've felt
- What you were forced to believe as a child by bullying adults who themselves had gotten lost
- What you've thought
- What you've said in the absence of self-knowledge
- What you've done in reaction to the world from your disconnected self

You are super-sexy life, beyond and unaffected by all these. When you accept your being as whole and complete, you feel better, think more clearly and constructively, speak with more kindness and more heart, and act more positively and with more compassion. All these enhance your sexiness.

When you commit to living your life that way, acceptance of others becomes easy and you can then assist them on their journey to wholeness and full inner enjoyment. You need social rules only as long as you don't live self-responsibly. You don't need social rules to keep you in line if you keep yourself in line. You don't need social rules to keep others in line when they keep themselves in line. Such a world is possible because its framework is embedded into your human nature. It always has been, from before the beginning of time. **Self-responsibility is sexy.**

Every day, through the ache of the disconnected heart that you feel, life calls your awareness to come home to it, where you feel cared for and unconditionally loved, no matter what you're feeling, thinking, saying or doing. Heed that call. Come home to life. Feel it nurture you. Feel it making you sexy. Feel it inspire and guide your thinking. Let inspired thinking guide your words and actions. **Coming home to life is sexy.**

In such a world, you create temporary rules as structures to more effectively reach goals that serve life, rather than forcing life to serve structures. Structures are meant to guide projects to completion. After completion, they can be dissolved, discarded or replaced by new structures for new projects. Trash structures when they no longer serve and are no longer needed. **Trashing unnecessary structures is sexy.**

The sacred heart needs no external social structures or rules imposed on it because it's the source of the natural flow of life in human form. **The sacred heart is sexy.** Fulfilled, your heart accepts what is, and can be free with other in the state of grace in which you were born and in which you live. Grace and freedom are everywhere present. They're absent only from the fantasy life of your imagination, memory and mind. Let go of the fantasy life, and accept your self as you really are. **Fulfillment is gracefully sexy.**

Unique Talents

Look around. Yours is an extremely diverse, complex, complicated human world. I'm in Los Angeles right now, in a hotel room, with desk and chair, toilet and TV, shower and windows, my computer and a cell phone that connects me to the rest of the world. I have Wi-Fi, wallpaper, mirrors, a sink, soap, shampoo, pictures and lamps. This is not a high-end hotel.

I hear traffic outside. There's a gas station next door. A paved road leads to LAX, the huge and technologically complex airport, whose workings I don't understand and could much less explain. Thousands of people serve in hundreds of capacities in what I described so far. Then there is the rest of the world, with all of the gadgets, applications and services.

What humans with different talents have built together in the past few hundred thousand years staggers imagination. Not all of it is good, but that's not the point here. The point is that human beings come with many unique talents and points of view that pooled, conceives and creates fantastic new worlds. **Pooling talents is sexy.** Each of you comes with unique talents that you can contribute to the whole.

What is your talent? Have you developed it? How far? Do you keep it secret and it helps no one, which is not sexy, or are you sharing it? What are its possible adverse effects? How can you lessen these? What cautions can you put in place?

Do you work with a team? **Teams and teamwork are sexy.** You manifest better when you work with others than when you work alone. I see it every day. Every meeting I attend reminds me. I think for myself. I'm smart, and I come up with smart ideas. And yet, every time I meet with others to look at one of my ideas, I find that other people bring other possibilities to them. Their perspectives are so different from the way I think that I'm shocked at the limits of my personal viewpoint of my project. It is enhancing, beneficial and sexy to invite other people on your team.

In the world you live in, competitive as it is, you sometimes hide your genius afraid that others want to steal it and knowing that some will. I've experienced that several times. But now I'm wise enough not to be angered but pleased by it. Imitation TRULY is the sincerest form of flattery. **Cooperation is sexy.**

One of my inventions has made it around the world, far broader than I could have ever done alone, simply because others stole it. Theft of ideas does not diminish me. It enhances me, and that's sexy. After all, thieves only steal what has value. In the end, it's about the contribution, not about my wish for recognition and money, both of which lose all meaning when life goes bye-bye and my body quits and dies.

Look around the world at inventions. You can name few of the inventors. Most died long ago, and no one remembers them. Do you think their inventions are now important to them? Wherever they are, they're not upset, and the living will continue to benefit from the contributions of these past sexy geniuses for ages to come. The inventors of anything that is more than a few centuries old have been forgotten, but their inventions 'live' on.

In social groups, your genius can find expression in ways where many benefit. That's sexy. It's nice but not necessary to be acknowledged. There's no better pat on the back than to see your gift made useful in the world. **Contribution is sexy**. In the end, your body craps out and you take only a full heart with you. Unshared and undeveloped, your secrets die with you. That's okay, too. Eventually, others will discover them anew.

The diverse talents that members bring to groups allow each to specialize and all to pool resources. This opens up a wide range of unique prospects that no member can create alone. With full acceptance and encouragement, each member of a social group brings more to benefit all. When members don't feel accepted and cherished, they will sometimes punish the group by keeping their best ideas to themselves. Members and individuals in groups do well to be aware of that. Are you aware of it regarding members of the groups you frequent? **Bringing help and benefits to others is sexy**.

Accept yourself, and bring your talents forward. It feels deep down really good and sexy, even when you don't receive the accolades that you desire. Let it go. Let your talents and efforts speak for themselves and for you. Take a deep breath, and remember that you are whole and that nothing can take your wholeness from you. When you forget, it's because your awareness wandered off. Bring it home. Get sexy again. Keep it home. Do your best. Your genius does not result from separation. It is your sexy gift from life to share with other lives. **Heart-felt genius is sexy**.

Price

What price do you pay for membership? Do you give up personal independence and freedom to become and remain a member? Why are you willing to do so? When you're only weakly committed and unaware that you most truly belong to life, you may use the group as a substitute to fulfill your need to belong. Not knowing how exactly to belong to life, you seek and choose an external group to attach yourself to.

You have to belong to something, you think. You look around and join with others who hold views similar to yours. After all, 'there's safety in numbers'. You fall in with them, and you have each other's backs. You begin to defend the notion of 'my group', which now takes precedence over following the internally known 'truth that makes you free'.

Many social problems begin with this shift from loyalty to truth into loyalty to group. If you know the truth that makes you free and stand up for that truth, your group might ostracize you. Then you'd be alone. A lot of people can't stand being alone. Alone, you go not to life but to anxiety or loneliness. To prevent that, you give up some of your integrity to rules of conduct imposed on you by the groups you join.

Are there groups that do NOT demand that kind of price? They exist, but they're rare. Most groups live into external agendas. Only rarely is a group's agenda to empower and encourage the internal experience of each member. Such groups tend to have a policy of openness. Group membership is not a key issue, simply because each member knows that s/he belongs to life. And yet, even though each one of you belongs to life, you live here with 8 billion other people. Accept that, and embrace and contribute to the existence of each one of them.

Your social group and other people can affect your health by their state of being, either in ways that improve, empower and enhance your sexy or in ways that tear it down. You've heard the expression, "You make me sick!" Maybe you've said it to someone who served as an emotional trigger in the heat of an argument. It confirms that we know how powerful the effect of others can be on us.

Build your own presence, and be comfortable and confident in it. The more strongly you remember to connect with life, the less dramatically others will affect you without your permission or agreement. The less connected you live to life, the more those around you affect your wellbeing. Unless or until you are strong in your self, know who among the people you know empowers and supports your growth. Keep mostly those people in your intimate circle and energy field. **Support and empowerment of others is sexy.** Empower and support them back.

Even when you are strong, some people may still be toxic for you and you may be wise to exclude them from your circle of daily interactions. However, avoiding such people does not mean that it's okay for you to hate them. People to avoid include

- 'Vampires' who drain your energy but chronically give nothing back
- Victims who insist on continuously reliving the memories of their past traumas and refuse to get back to living life
- Those who incessantly complain but are not committed to fix what they complain about
- Those who non-stop criticize you and others and for whom nothing you do is ever good enough

Even more important, however, make time alone with yourself to get as close to your unshakeable self-presence as you can. Become so strong in your inner experience of life that you can stay in your power even in the presence of vampires, complainers, victims and critics. When you fall in love with the feeling of life, no one can make you fall out of love with it, no matter what. **Falling in love with the feeling of life is sexy.**

Inspiring complainers is sexy. If you can't help them, create distance or fire them from your circle to give them time and space to find the beauty of their inner presence, too. When their old, sad 'stories' stop working because no one listens to them anymore, they may discover their sexy life and create better, more uplifting new stories to tell.

In high-functioning social groups, most members are strong in their individual presence and contribute presence to the entire group. They accept each other as unique, gifted and valued. They hold space to allow each member to contribute, and accept each member's gifts with gratitude. They don't shy away from setting straight those members who hide their gifts or steal the gifts of others. What do you bring to the social groups of which you are a member? **Strong group members are sexy.**

Pressure

When you are not in touch with the wholeness that comes from the feeling of belonging to life, you are vulnerable to social manipulation. Others can deceive, coerce or bully you to submit to their specific personal or social agenda. It's not a good situation to be in and underscores the need to make time to connect with the core of your being. In your sexy presence and power and with a bit of practice, it becomes easier to stand your ground when someone pressures you. **Standing up for yourself and life is sexy.**

Belonging should not require you to be someone other than your natural self.

Who do you have to pretend to be to get along with a mate, friend or group? Don't pretend. Phony is obvious and decidedly not sexy. Being who you are and feeling the confidence inherent in being your natural self is sexy. If you have friends, lovers and groups for whom you have to fake it to belong, replace them with people who appreciate you as you are. You can be honest with such friends and group members and that's both healthy and sexy. **Appreciation is sexy.**

Groups that accept the uniqueness of their members are

sexy. Only join groups like that. The pressure to belong takes many forms other than bullying. People may shun, threaten, admonish or exclude you. They may deny you rights and privileges. They may deceive and take unfair advantage of you. They might temporarily banish you to try to make you fall in line. They might gang up on you with others. Banishment is a gift in such situations because it gives you back your life. **Personal standards are sexy.**

Membership requires contribution. You have to help the group in some way. Some groups, before they let you join will ask you, "What do you bring?" Think about what you CAN bring and then commit to bringing it. Living with others requires giving something of your self. **Pulling your weight is sexy.** Do more for the common good than is expected of you. Give freely without insisting on getting something back. Do not freeload on the goodwill of the group and its members. Help where you can. Being a member of a group can enrich your life and make it easier and safer. Give in kind. When all members do what they can for the group, starting with being present and self-responsible, group membership is an external extension to the internal blessings that come with being life.

How can you disconnect from social pressure? Begin by knowing that something within you is already (and has always been) beyond social pressure and will always be free of it. You can't be pressured when, with practice, you can stay calmly in the being you are.

Social pressure can't get to your central core. You are free in that core even when your body is being pushed or pulled around, negative words are used, and others speak to you in demanding or demeaning tones. It's good to believe that this place exists within you, but it's much better to find, feel and live in that powerful place. **Standing up calmly to social pressure is sexy.**

Let me tell you a story about a personal learning that involved going to jail for 30 days. In a court case, I refused to obey the order of a judge to pay money because I felt it was unfair, and told him that I wouldn't pay. He threatened me with 30 days in jail if I did not pay within 45 days and I said I'd take the jail time. On the day he had said he'd put me in jail, I turned myself in. He then told me he'd give me more time to pay. I insisted that he put me in jail as he had promised. He had no choice but to do that.

In jail, I had a blast with other inmates and guards by simply treating everyone with respect. After my release, the judge started up again. I told him he could put me in jail again, I would enjoy myself again, and that it would cost the government a bundle of dollars again to keep and feed me there for a month. At that point, he became reasonable and stopped bullying me. **Treating people with respect is sexy.**

Eventually, all the issues of the case were resolved but it was in accordance with my sense of integrity. What did I learn from this experience? The moment you lose your fear of losing your freedom, the group loses its power over you. In other words, when you know life so deeply that you lose your fear of not belonging, you're forever free in your life to do what needs to be done. **Courage under threat is sexy.**

In one way or another, your body will wear out, so be clear from your heart and in your mind what's worth wearing yourself out for. Ask yourself, "For what purpose will I gladly use up my body?" Make it a purpose that protects and cares for life, body and planet. Or make it something else. It's your choice. What you choose defines your quality of life.

Behavior

The psychologist Alfred Adler suggested making a distinction between people, who are worth caring for, and unacceptable behavior, which has to be addressed. **Addressing unacceptable behavior is sexy.** "I love you but your behavior is unacceptable, and I expect you to change it for the better in the following way." It helps to be clear. "I'm not looking for an apology. I AM looking for a change in behavior."

The distinction between human beings who are worth loving, and behavior that must stop, is also present in religious writing. "Hate the sin, but love the sinner," reads a passage from the New Testament. **Separating the value of people from the quality of their behavior is sexy.** You're not your behavior or the words, thoughts and feelings that framed your behavior. You are life. Life unconditionally loves your body, and also powers all your thoughts and emotions. None of these affect life, which always remains whole, pure and light.

Love all members of your groups as they are but address any behaviors that threaten group safety, coherence and ability to thrive. As a member of groups, you can modify some of your behaviors, if it makes sense to you, to align with the group without having to become someone you're not.

As life, you are and each member is the highest common denominator. Life is the glue that keeps the group harmonious, cohesive and moving forward in the same direction. Life powers all steps of all members toward shared constructive goals. As life, you can play your part to keep members inspired.

Here's a cautionary consideration. Before you commit time and energy to a group or a relationship, find out how they deal with disagreement. When you say, "No!" you quickly find out how individuals and groups deal with conflict. You also learn how much need for control they have. Don't join groups that have a low tolerance for differences in opinions and new or out-of-the-box ideas, unless you're comfortable being controlled.

Skip groups whose members insist on suppressing your spontaneous expressions and who value controlling their members more than their members' uniqueness. You'll be amazed how intensely members and some groups will coerce you to adopt a rigid culture and specific ways of speaking and acting. It's a warning sign. In the world of mastery and masters (the topic of Chapter 13), truly free speech exists. **Freedom of expression is delightfully sexy.** Each person is on a unique inner journey. Each experiences his or her personal level of knowledge of self and world. Each one shares her or his personal expression of that individual journey of discovery in a unique way. As many different ways to express experiences exist as there are individuals in the group.

Self-actualized people all speak in personal 'incorrect' ways, spontaneously, without memorized sets of stories, texts and explanations. They don't stick to only a few limited scripts. They encourage you to convey your own experiences uniquely, and welcome you to give voice to your own heart, feelings and thoughts. It's a joy to hear two such people describe their discoveries of life in inspired personal ways.

Masters of self-knowledge foster accepting, encouraging, lit-up learning environments. **Insightful originality is sexy**. Those who focus on their inner life often come up with profound insights. They talk in different ways using different words, yet they understand each other. They feel the wonder of utterances without getting stuck on words.

You're lucky to find a group in which all members are equally cared for and respected. No one deserves more respect than anyone else. Each person leads her or his own life. One master, life, is present in each member of the group, 8 billion in all. Each person has access to and lives by the built-in wisdom of life.

Your actions express your state of being. **Constructive states of being are sexy**. The conduct of a group shows the collective total of the states of being of its members. Discontent leads to destructive behavior. Behavior that originates in contentment is more likely to be constructive.

Alfred Adler said that every human being's innermost striving is "to move from a felt minus to a felt plus, a striving for perfection, and a striving for God-likeness." Human beings will do anything to try to fulfill that innermost striving. Adler, who died in 1937, did not spell out the origin of that striving and how exactly to fulfill it.

Now, much more knowledge on this subject is available. We have access to almost unlimited facts and information. From my personal journey and those of others, I can tell you. The striving Adler talked about is also known as wanting to feel whole, complete, content or in peace. It's the burn to feel internally connected to life. That is your most powerful innermost driving force. You'll chase it everywhere in the world, but you'll not find it outside of you. Feeling whole, perfection and God-likeness are *personal internal encounters.*

In searching for God-likeness externally, you may become an autocrat or despot who assumes human laws and rules don't apply to you, and do immoral, corrupt or unlawful acts. Unsatisfied striving explains why power corrupts, and why it can lead to the kinds of serious social consequences in cultures, religions and nations that news media focus on. That's how strong a drive it is.

When a discontent populace deposes a tyrant, many expect social justice, equality and democracy to automatically take its place. That's a pipe dream. It hardly ever happens. Why? Discontent people don't come together in harmony. They are more likely to riot because they know what they DON'T want but they don't know what they DO want.

Why do people remain discontent after the dictator is gone? The answer is that no nation, culture or religion systematically shows people how to access feeling whole within their own being. They may have words about it but don't provide a method for getting you to that feeling. Without contentment and rulers to control them, disaffected people create the chaos, violence and brutality to express their discontent.

Another consideration of social groups involves looking at the nature of their books of rules and constitutions.

First, all sets of rules and all constitutions are flawed documents. Why? They're flawed because they're products of human minds, which are by nature dual and split the world. Documents, laws, rules, words and thoughts create conflict: for or against. They don't bring you heart-felt feelings of oneness: peace, wholeness, perfection, or contentment. They don't unify. They separate and divide.

In fact, while your heart and life is 100% for you, your mind and the thoughts it creates are 50% for you and 50% against you. The realm of thoughts and documentation is the realm of passionate arguments that create contentious politicians and citizens. Even voting divides groups into opposing factions of winners and losers. Consensus decision-making works better. It's more heart-felt and does not split groups.

Second, even if the intent of the people who create documents, constitutions, laws and rules is lofty and noble, they can't transfer this lofty and noble intent to the people they are meant to guide or control, or even to those whom they hire to administer them. Content people use documents in good and creative ways. Discontent people apply the same documents in mean and destructive ways. Written documents of rules and laws themselves can't make people content or discontent.

Do you see the dilemma? Rules don't ensure wisdom or insight. **Insight and wisdom are sexy.** Rulers must impose and enforce rules on subjects. It's why they engender resentment, resistance and rebellion. Eventually, people get fed up and revolt.

It gets worse. The people who service institutions don't do so according to the high-minded intent of their founders but according to their own state of being in the moment. They have good days and bad days and they too need to be threatened and controlled by fear to try to force them to 'properly' carry out their job roles. But threat and force do not lead staff to insights and wisdom.

Here's the bottom line. In the history of humanity, no group ever developed or educated members into full presence of their lit up inner state of being on a national, institutional, workplace or educational level. Without competence to systematically teach such self-mastery skills, you lack a reliable way to develop strong, self-responsible members or citizens. If you lack these, how will you get strong, self-responsible men, women, parents, children, families, workers, bosses, educators and so on?

It's like trying to create a peaceful world without peaceful people. That's not possible. With globally available knowledge and communications technology, self-mastery can now be taught and learned in a deliberate, consistent and practical way. **Self-mastery is sexy.** You want 8 billion people to live in peace and harmony together with everyone's basic needs met? Teach them the nature of their human nature. It's my mission to help bring that about.

Western civilization, culture, government and religion were built largely on the insights and teachings of two masters, Socrates and Christ, and on efforts to understand and live by these teachings of self-knowledge for self-mastery. Educated, 'powerful' people have also misused these teachings to control less educated, less powerful 'subjects'. Over time, increasingly materialistic cultures dilute and discard these teachings. Then their institutions lose ground, and people move toward chaos.

Eastern and Middle Eastern civilizations, also based on masters and inner wisdom teachings, are also being eroded by materialism, by the frantic pace of modern lifestyles, and by neglect and pride. The answer isn't to more forcefully impose old outdated teachings, but to embody the true substance and essence of what those original masters taught: self-responsible self-knowledge in the service of self-mastery. Get to know nature and human nature more deeply, and make that knowledge part of folk wisdom. Widely teach it by all possible means throughout our now global village and culture.

Discontent people sometimes use institutional power to treat those they're hired to serve as less worthy than they are. When these people learn to act with only the power of their heart as their protection, they'll treat others with care as equals.

Life made all of us equal. We are not the same, but we are equally worthy of respect. Re-discover and embrace, as an individual, the insights and teachings of the lit up masters who were the sexiest of all people to ever live. Commit yourself to your personal mastery of what these masters mastered. Without it, you head toward the destruction of nature, social groups, families, yourself and your future.

This also applies to banks, capitalist enterprises and governments, the global powers and dictatorships of our time.

These all work perfectly if those in charge of them love all of life and nature, and commit themselves to protect, care for and assist ALL citizens of the world. **Generosity is sexy.** When they do not love and serve all, they contribute to abuse and enslavement of the people who create their affluence.

Greed involves theft (confiscation) of nature's and of life's gifts, and getting more for your self by giving less and taking more from others. No matter whether you're a slave or slave owner in this autarchy, you become highly sexy when you conquer the hold that banks and money have on your mind. A mind made up to serve life is sexy. True, that's easier said than done. Everything is easier said than done, but anything is possible.

When you're wise enough to use money and power to serve life, you can be trusted with a lot of money. **Serving life is sexy.** As long as you're discontent, money can be destructive in your hands. Until you feel fully present and content, your fellow citizens can trust you with only enough money to take care of your basic survival needs.

Bottom line: The state of being that you cultivate, as an individual, is either the sexiest and most important gift or the most dismal curse you bring to this planet.

Never underestimate your power to cultivate sexy self-responsible presence. **You are sexy when you right wrongs, correct mistakes, admit errors and learn from failures.** These take self-knowledge, courage and humility, which make you powerfully sexy.

Your Word

To complete the chapter on social health, consider the importance of your word. In most situations, you are a free agent, free to give or to withhold your word. You can promise, commit or agree to something, or you can say 'No!' to it. You're free to make an oral or written contract, or you can turn it down.

When you discuss making an agreement or contract, you consider delivering something to another, and the other promises to deliver something to you. After discussion, both sides come to a verbal agreement; they commit it to writing; they read and modify it for greater clarity if necessary; after reading, further discussion and more modification, they agree on a final written version that accurately reflects their understanding. Then they both sign the contract. After that, they carry out their duties, as specified in the contract. When you sign an agreement or contract, you choose to no longer be a free agent. You bind yourself to another, and commit to honor the terms of your agreement.

Your word—giving, honoring and restoring it—is the single most important social issue of all time. You've promised another that s/he can depend on you to perform. Others depend on you delivering what you agreed on. They invest time and money on the expectation of your promised performance. Not being able to depend on keeping the agreements people make with one another make cooperative projects impossible. That is why giving and honoring your word is so important. **Making and keeping promises is sexy.** By your word, you enter into a sacred trust with others.

Living and surviving in a hostile world depend on you honoring that trust. Successful thriving and teamwork depend on team members keeping the promises they make. In other words, honoring your word is vital both as warrior in terms of survival and as sage in terms of progress.

All actions and interactions have consequences. By your word, you agree to fulfill your promise to do your part of the combined effort toward common goals for mutual benefit.

Your word is the law you create and agree to live by, and you are never above that law. The power and importance of obeying your law by keeping your word can't be overstated. Legally, it's why breach of trust or contract is a big deal, and why courts of law have rules about breach of contract, breach of trust and unjust enrichment in place. It's why they punish the 'breacher' and reward the 'breachee' with triple damages, and add the costs of legal defense, as well as lost time, sales and opportunities. Giving your word is not a trivial matter. **When you embody your word as your law, you're sexy.**

By keeping your agreements, you earn others' trust, build a reputation for reliability, and create powerful relationships that enable you to carry out great projects. **Honoring your agreements is sexy.** Once you give your word, it binds you even if you claim that you did so without due deliberations. Breaking your word when more interesting, profitable or shinier possibilities come along saddles you personally, relationally and financially.

Breaking your word and trust is the cardinal social sin. Why do people do it? Why does anyone break an agreement after making it? The answer is that it is easier to make an agreement than to honor it, especially in moments of challenge, temptation or personal discontent. These lead to deliberate thinking focused on finding ways to skirt your word in order to get more for your self. This can lead to exploiting, taking unfair advantage or cheating your partner. There are respectful ways of ending or changing contracts, none of which involve breach, exploitation, cheating, bullying or lying.

In a world where many people value money more than life, it's most often greed—the love of money—that leads to breach of contract. Check in with yourself. See if this is true for you. I'm willing to be wrong. In fact, I'd love to be wrong. Observe how it works within your mind and in relation with your heart—your better angels, as some people say. This is important homework for each of us to do.

Breach of agreement puts everything and everyone in jeopardy. By going back on your word, you create mistrust that damages relationships. You foster disappointment, anger, and grief. You create suspicion, enmity, conflict and even war. You've probably heard the common laments about broken promises: 'But you gave your word!!' 'You promised, but you broke your promise!!' 'We had a contract, but you went back on it!!' 'We made an agreement, but then you lied to me!!' 'I can't trust you anymore.' Breach the biggest bad social deal.

Recall events in your life, both from your side and from that of others, where breach of agreement or contract led to serious bad feeling-based problems. Heartfelt honesty, or a return to honoring an existing contract on the part of the one who breached it avoids or repairs the bad feelings and the trust problems that stem from it.

Unavoidable breach: What happens when you give your word with best intentions and a commitment to keep it and follow through, but events beyond your control conspire to make it impossible to keep your word? That occasionally happens. How do you deal with it? The answer is not obvious only because many people are not principled in their social interactions. They may blow off their broken promise as if it meant nothing, hoping to 'get away with it'. They deny the consequences of breaking their agreement on those they made it to, and pretend or rationalize that it's okay. It's NOT okay.

When you know that you will not keep a promise you made, let the other know as soon as you know. Ask them to tell you how you can make it right. What damage to them has your breach caused? How do you repair that damage? How can you rebuild the broken trust? It will cost you something in time, energy, humble pie, or money. **Repairing the damage done by breaking your promise is sexy**. This can often re-establish the trust you broke, and you might even be able to strengthen the relationship and the trust by taking it on.

When you DO have to break a promise, don't be dismissive about it. Honor the person. Honor the trust between you. Honor the relationship. Honor the agreement. Appreciate and acknowledge that your breach incurred a cost on those to whom you made the promise, and take responsibility to make good on the agreement you broke. **Honoring the person, trust, agreement and relationship is sexy**. Return to delivering on promises after you break them. It feels right, and you grow when you talk straight and walk straight. When you fail or refuse to restore broken agreements, you damage yourself as a human being.

Breaking your word for personal gain is cowardly and heartless. You shrink as a person because you lose your connection to your wholeness. You sacrifice your life energy and freedom. You choose to value something else more than your life and your agreement, as well as your partner. Imagine! You sell out your life, the only real treasure here, for money.

Our word, which is both promise and agreement, is the only thread that connects us with others. We achieve lofty, noble, heartfelt or glorious goals together only as long as that thread remains unbroken. It breaks only when we choose to break it. Feeling discontent leads to negative thoughts, which power disloyal actions.

Our word with others is vitally important whenever we have crises or possibilities that are bigger than what we can handle alone, and that need more than one hand on deck.

When your word's based on full presence in all of your being, you and your trust-based team can accomplish any goal to which you set your mind. Your efforts can then benefit and lighten the lives of all those you touch.

7

ENVIRONMENTAL HEALTH:
Alignment with Nature

Beauty

ALIGNMENT WITH NATURE AND THE natural environment is the seventh key part of total sexy health designed by nature. When you think about it, you realize that all of 'ordinary' life is by its nature extraordinary and sexy when lived with in-the-moment awareness. **All of fresh, raw, living nature is sexy.** The wildness of nature is sexy. You're filled with sexy and surrounded by it.

Alignment with nature is sexy. Sunlight is the sexy power on this planet. Cool air and sunshine on wet leaves after rain are sexy. Light is sexy, and even darkness is sexy if you're the light in that darkness. The constant play of colors, outlines and movements is sexy. The warmth of the sun, and the smell of freshly sun-drenched and tanned skin are sexy.

Fresh air, negative ions near a waterfall, and the smell of ozone after lightning, rain and thunder are sexy. Wind and clouds are sexy. A cool breeze on your skin is sexy. Blue sky is sexy. The wind in the willows is sexy. Breathing is sexy. Oxygen is sexy. The thin envelope of air that surrounds our planet is sexy.

Fresh, cold water is refreshingly sexy. Icebergs in the arctic are sexy. A waterfall, rapids and gurgling creeks are sexy. Raging rivers, still lakes, waves and surf are sexy. The reflection of light on eddies and waves crashing on a beach are sexy. Rain in the desert is sexy. Dew on the grass in the morning is sexy. Steam issuing from volcanic vents is sexy. Hailstones bouncing on a tin roof are sexy.

Craggy, snow-capped mountaintops are sexy. **Bare round rocks are sexy.** Moist soil and desert sands are sexy. Earth used for potting plants is sexy. Rocks supply sexy minerals. Canyons, caves and rock formations are sexy. Gems and crystals are sexy. Clay in a potter's hands is sexy.

Living creatures are sexy. Microbes that protect and clean up the environment are sexy. **Everything about green plants is sexy: roots, stems, leaves and seeds.** Flowers and their fragrances are sexy. The shapes of leaves are sexy. A thousand shades of green are sexy. Growth is sexy. Adaptation to environment is sexy. Grasses, shrubs and trees are sexy. Trunks, branches and the silhouettes of plants are sexy. All of the animals, from jellyfish to monkeys are sexy. Even spiders and snakes are sexy. Dogs, cats and other pets are sexy. Cows and horses (especially horses) are sexy. Human beings are sexy.

You get the picture. **Everything in nature is sexy in and by its nature.**

Dangerous Resources

Sunlight, air, water and Earth (including creatures) provide you with all of the resources you need, but can also destroy you. They demand your respect. **Respect for nature is sexy.** Nature provides material for food, clothing, shelter and companionship; it can also poison, sting, infect, kill and eat you.

As sexy as sun, air, water, Earth, microbes, plants, animals and humans are, they're also dangerous. Too little sun will pale you and too much sun can scorch you. A nuclear furnace far from Earth in space, the sun is the right distance away to optimize biological benefits and to minimize its bio-destructive potential. **The 'Goldilocks' distance from the sun for living creatures, where you are, is sexy.** Further out, you'd freeze and further in, you'd cook to death.

Additional protection from the sun, which air and atmosphere provide, is part of the sexy Goldilocks zone. Even so, naked creature, you're vulnerable to burns by sun's more savage rays unless you cover up. Hair (mammals), feathers (birds), scales (snakes) and exoskeleton (insects, spiders) protect most animals. Sexy plants stand naked in the sun all day, but don't get burned. They use sunlight energy to make antioxidants that shield them from the damage that the sun could do.

If there is too little air, the sun burns you. If there's too much air, too little sunlight will reach you. If there is too much oxygen, you burn up. Too little oxygen, and you choke to death. **A small, sexy margin of oxygen in breathing air keeps you alive.** The plants that are alive right now produce only a fraction of that oxygen. Plants in the past made three quarters of it. Being buried underground, they could not rot, and so they left the oxygen they made while living, in our breathing atmosphere above the ground. Now, we dig them up—as fossil fuels—and burn them for energy at faster and faster rates. Each carbon atom we burn takes two atoms of oxygen out of your breathing air.

My car burns 500-700 times more oxygen than my body uses in the time I drive it. We're burning oxygen faster than plants can replenish it. Unsustainable. **Water, wind and solar energy are sexy**. They don't burn up the oxygen we need to breathe to live. Hang on to, and save, the oxygen that animals and we must have to live. Develop non-carbon sustainable energy sources. Without oxygen, your lights go out in seconds and you die in minutes. Too little oxygen, and animals and humans perish.

All living creatures depend for life on water. All microbes, plants, animals and humans must have it to live. Without water, you're dead in about a week. Fresh water makes up less than

2% of the total water on this planet. Half of it is accessible to us. **Intelligent global water management is sexy.** It's one of the most urgent and beneficial projects of our time. It can solve many major global problems including drought, hunger and the deaths of adults as well as children. Life absorbs into your body 20+ times more water than the total of all nutrients.

Rocks, earth and soils are source of 18 essential minerals. Plants use these, plus water, carbon dioxide and sunlight to manufacture essential vitamins and fatty acids, as well as proteins, starches, sugars, fiber and thousands of other molecules you need, and even the oxygen you breathe. **All plants are sexy.**

Dangers from sunlight include sunburn, blisters and skin cancers. Dangers from the air include the damage done by windstorms like hurricanes, tornadoes, snowstorms and blizzards. Dangers from water can be widespread, and includes floods, droughts, rising ocean levels and sinking ground water tables. It also involves avalanches, tsunamis, currents, and undertows. Water can cause hypothermia and drowning. Hailstones, icebergs and crevasses in glaciers are also dangerous. Dangers from Earth include rockslides, sand storms and volcanoes, plus earthquakes and dust blockage of the sun.

As part of nature, human beings can also be resources or dangers. They can protect, care for and encourage you, which is sexy. They can deceive and steal from you, and injure or destroy your body. I'm sure you've had your share of dangerous experiences with people. Among creatures, humans have the greatest capacity to confuse, mislead and take advantage of (exploit) others. It's not sexy to do that. The good news is that when you live fully present in your whole being, you feel so rich that you'll be far less tempted to exploit, and you'll be far less vulnerable to others who try to do it.

Feeling rich and fulfilled is sexy. When you feel like you have everything, which you do, you're less interested in more stuff, because you don't need more stuff. Feeling life's care for you protects you against exploitation. You won't so easily fall for a bum's rush or hustle when you know that you already have more than everything you need.

Respect & Appreciation

With wonder and awe, behold the thousands of facets of nature's beauty. Your greatest talent, unique to humans is your ability to enjoy and admire, which is super-sexy. When you slow down enough to notice, you feel overwhelming gratitude for what you've been given, both within and around you. **Feeling grateful is sexy.** Life gave you a planet to do something with. This is your planet, your country and your government. It's your city, your neighborhood and your house. You own your family, children, body and a lot more. You own a lot!! You own all these to meet your needs, and beyond that, to delight in the fact of their existence. What are you doing with all that you own?

Ownership to enjoy is sexy. Ownership to enjoy is a unique and different kind of title. It's non-exclusive: You have no papers to keep others from also enjoying the non-exclusive title you have to what you own. It's non-possessive: You share the world you own with all others who all also own it. It's temporary: You own it only in moments in which you focus on and enjoy what you non-exclusively and non-possessively own.

Appreciate and be grateful for the countless gifts of nature in the form of resources. Imagine you were thirsty but there was no water. That would be cruel. But nature gave you thirst and provided water for you to drink. Imagine you were hungry but there was no food. That would be unfair, but nature gave you hunger and provided food for you to eat (except when heartless hoarders deprive you of it, or you're on a cleansing fast).

Imagine you needed to breathe but there was no oxygen. That'd be unthinkable, but nature gave you the need to breathe and provided the oxygen that satisfies your need. Imagine you were naked and cold but there was no clothing. That would be punitive, but nature made you naked and provided materials from which to make clothes to keep you warm.

Imagine you were vulnerable but there was no protection from storms and wild animals. That would be rejection and abandonment, but nature considered your vulnerability and provided materials for shelter.

Many other sexy stories could be told about nature creating your needs and providing the resources to fulfill them.

Nature's power is sexy and commands respect. This is not negotiable. Nature is powerful, but you can learn her ways and laws and can then respectfully harness her for your benefit. In that way, though powerful, nature is super-generous. Just a few of hundreds of sexy ways in which nature serves humans:

- Sunlight, air, and water for energy
- Earth, air, and water to transport goods
- Water, earth and sunlight for growing food
- Wind and wings for airborne flight
- Gravity for sports like diving and skiing
- Heat and chemicals for killing pathogens
- Fire for clay pots, metal tools, light and warmth
- Electromagnetism for signal and power transmission
- Glass for lenses, magnification and starting fires

Everything we've created that constitutes civilization is based on understanding nature. **Nature's laws are sexy.** Aligning with those laws, we have made them useful. We have moved from

- Survival to thriving
- Eking out a miserable existence to having creative leisure time
- Living in ignorance or superstition to discovering the sexy nature of what is within and around us everywhere.

- Living isolated in cold caves to being globally in touch through hot media, no matter where we live

Nature's Cycles

Nature's cycles are sexy. Everything in nature moves in cycles. Nature re-cycles and re-uses everything. Night follows your day and day follows your night. Your day is for activity and your night is for rest. You follow and live more or less adapted to this cycle 365 times each year, usually for 100 years or less. **Aligned with nature's cycles, you live a healthy = sexy life.** Out of line, you live less long, less healthy and less sexy.

Spring follows winter. Summer follows spring. Autumn follows summer. Winter follows fall. Every year, the seasons flow. Winter, a time of death, darkness, cold and rest, turns into spring, a time of new growth, flowering and renewal. Summer, a time of fruit and seed maturity, precedes a time of harvest, aging and rage against the dying of the light.

The weather also follows (somewhat crooked) cycles. Dry follows wet follows dry. Storm follows calm follows storm. Heat follows cold follows heat. The wind blows east. The wind blows west. Sometimes it goes around in circles.

Fresh water evaporates from the salty ocean, forms clouds blown over land by winds, drops as rain and then finds its way, by gravity, back to the ocean, where the unending water cycle starts again. **The water cycle is sexy.** In its cycling, water paints the planet green, grows foods, serves for drink, hygiene and recreation, replenishes water tables in the ground, provides transportation and serves as a source of energy.

Plants and animals follow the **sexy carbon dioxide-oxygen cycle.** Plants turn carbon dioxide, a waste product from chemical reactions (more recently, the breath of animals; most recently from burning fossil fuels), along with water, minerals and the energy of sunlight, into sugars. Oxygen is the waste product that plants exhale from this reaction. Their waste, oxygen, is the vital principle in your breathing air. You breathe in oxygen and eat the plants, and in your body they react together to produce carbon dioxide that you exhale, water that you filter out, and energy that moves the chemical wheels of all of your activity. The energy dissipates. Water goes back in the ground. The carbon dioxide, your waste, becomes food for plants in a perpetual cycle of plant and animal interdependence. In this cycle, plants are the superior partners. They do not need you for carbon dioxide, but you need them for oxygen. It's one reason to revere plants like they were gods. They can happily live without you, but you depend on them for everything.

Rocks break down into soils. Soils feed plants to make food. You eat food, extract water and nutrients from it, and discard un-useful remains of food back into the soil. Here they become food to eat again, nutrients and water to absorb again, and remains to return to soil again. This is the **sexy food-soil cycle**.

We interrupt this cycle at our peril. We eat food, deplete soil, and instead of replenishing soil with our wastes, flush wastes, which are soil, into rivers and oceans. Land becomes increasingly less fertile and the capacity of soils and fields to grow foods deteriorates more every year.

What I'm about to suggest may sound strange, but it makes sense in practice. Normally, we cook our food and flush our waste. There's a nature-friendlier way. Eat foods in their most nutritious way: fresh, whole, raw, and organic. Dry and cook wastes to kill viruses, bacteria and parasites (no, not on your stove, silly!!). Return the cooked wastes to the land to turn them back into the soil they were before plants turned them into foods we ate and turned into wastes. That way, soils remain productive and fertile, we eat more nutritious foods, our rivers don't become sewage-polluted, we save energy because we produce less waste than the total weight of the food we eat, and we complete the natural food-soil cycle. It's a major project that awaits clearer thought and greater love for life, nature and planet. **Fertile, productive soils are sexy.**

The life-death cycle is sexy. Everything in your body is naturally made from earth, water and oxygen, the body building blocks, and from sunlight, the power source. Every day, your body runs on sunlight energy stored in bonds between atoms. Life pulls into the body oxygen from the air you breathe, water that you drink, and nutrients from the foods you eat.

If you weigh 154 pounds (average adult weight; men more and women less), and you live 100 years, life sucks up into your body about 4 tons of nutrients. These include the proteins, fats/oils and carbs, and the minerals, vitamins, and nucleic acids that you eat, digest and absorb. You don't absorb fiber. You absorb about 18 tons of oxygen in that lifetime of 100 years. You absorb about 100 tons of water.

What happens to all that stuff? All of it's recycled. Oxygen becomes carbon dioxide and plants turn it back into oxygen. Water leaves the body via sweat, urine, breath and stool, and goes back into the water cycle. All food molecules and minerals go back to the soil on land or into rivers, lakes and oceans. Nature recycles everything.

The atoms that made up your body will end up in plants, animals, other human beings and microbes. Scientists say that with each breath, you take in a few atoms of oxygen that Genghis Khan, a moose in Canada a thousand years ago and Socrates once breathed. A nameless cave man, Lord Ram, your neighbor's ancestors and Marco Polo once breathed in some of them. An unremembered warrior of old, Jesus Christ and the Queen of Sheba once inhaled a few atoms of the oxygen that you now breathe. In this way, your body is intimate with almost everyone who's ever lived here in the past.

The minerals that move through your body end up in tomatoes, carrots, potatoes and broccoli, in beans and squash, in bread and meat that your neighbors, their neighbors and their pets eat. A few molecules of the water that you drink and absorb during your lifespan will end up in millions of people around the world. In this way, you're intimately connected to all other creatures that will live here in the future: people, plants, animals and microbes. **The kinship of all living creatures is sexy**. We're all made of the same materials, perpetually recycled by nature. You have reason to celebrate every moment and every day. Celebrate it! **Celebration is sexy.**

Sustainability

Imagination without heart and discipline is half a gift and half a curse. Through imagination, human beings became the most powerful species on this planet. We invented ways to live and created civilizations, methods of travel, ways to communicate and gadgets of every kind for greater convenience.

Our imagination also made us the most dangerous creature to ever exist. Together, we created most of the most serious problems on this planet. Why? What is our problem? We live more in fantasy than in reality. We work more for banks than for life, in spite of the fact that life's the only REAL wealth here.

We've cut ourselves off from nature and painted nature as an enemy to be defeated and exploited rather than a friend to be cherished. We take what nature gave to us as a gift, claim ownership of it, fudge it up, and then sell it back to others for money and power. We leave destruction and messes wherever we go. We don't clean up after ourselves.

We erected a statue of Liberty in New York and we honor the freedom it symbolizes, but we built no balancing statue of Responsibility in Los Angeles. We fight to maintain our freedom without accepting responsibility. We take the money we got from selling nature and run. We leave nature and other people to clean up after us. This is not sustainable.

Sustainability is our long-term promise to our children and future generations that they'll be able to live on the same quality planet as we did. We constantly break this promise. Keeping the promise requires us to restore each place we change by our activity to its original state. That's easier said than done. Talk is cheap, but sustainability involves a lot of work. **A truly sustainable planet is sexy.** Reversing the toll that our interference with nature creates takes time, effort and deliberate care. Treating symptoms without addressing root causes keeps us perpetually busy, because we never actually fix our problems. "Action should lead to inaction (completion)," said the Chinese sage Lao Tse. **Action that leads to completion is sexy.** Action that requires us to take more action is not. Eventually, we fail to fix what we wrecked.

We already know that the natural planet, in spite of all our talk about technology and human ingenuity, is getting worse for those who live on it. It may not be worse in terms of finances, but it's worse in terms of the health of land and oceans, of climate change, and of the loss of species. We also see it in terms of stress, frustration, confusion and mental problems, and of degenerative conditions and habitats, which are symptoms of living in unsustainable ways.

The greatest danger in your personal world is your personal *ignore-ance*: what needs you attention that you ignore. The greatest danger in the world is the sum of our collective ignorance. We can't fix the internal and external problems to which we don't pay attention or acknowledgement. **Knowledge of both nature and of self is sexy.** We benefit from knowing more of the natural world within which we live and the world of our inner nature.

Sustainability takes deliberate living. Take what you need. Share what you have and don't need. Don't waste. Do everything you do with awareness and care, and without undue destruction. Don't destroy a creature just to see it die. Commit to eat what you kill. Complete the natural cycles. Clean up your messes. Clean up the pollution that ignorant people, industries and governments left behind. **Sustainability is sexy.**

Hold yourself, others, industries & institutions to account for the consequences of your and their actions. **Accountability is sexy.** Make sure what you do benefits all without hurting any. Live consciously. Especially, live self-aware, knowing you were born whole, missing nothing and rich inside with everything. Know that you need only to meet your simple needs for air, water, food, clothing, shelter, love, joy and acceptance. You don't need stuff for prestige to brag about and show off.

Act aware of the fact that life is the only hot commodity on this planet. Be clear that just because you CAN do something does not mean that you SHOULD do it. Before you act, anticipate and address the consequences of your actions. If what you intend to do does not protect, care for and enrich life and peace, don't do it. **Living lit up from within is sexy.** Live in harmony with others and with nature. Feel fulfilled and serve life, giving of your light in whatever ways you can, to help others also live full, lit up lives. Most of your work is homework. It's work to do at home within your own awareness.

Industry

This planet, nature, and its creatures were here long before human imagination created industries. It is important to remember that. Your ancestors survived and even thrived without the techno-gadgets and distractions you now consider indispensable. Says who? Think of it this way. According to those who study natural history, living creatures began to adorn the planet about 4.3 billion years ago. All presently living creatures developed from the original ones.

In nature's living play, any creature unable to adapt to the existing natural system was not fit to live, and nature discarded and recycled it before reproduction. It therefore left no descendants. The fact that you exist in the thin slice of time called 'NOW' means that you survived and inherited the wisdom of countless generations, in an unbroken line of biological successes that goes all the way back to the beginning. **Your long, unbroken heritage is sexy**. Be humbled by and proud of that heritage. Most of it happened in the absence of industry. Nature can live without industry but industry completely depends on nature and can't exist without it. Accept this hierarchy.

Industry is impossible without nature. **Industry subservient to nature is sexy**. If industry hurts nature, discard, re-think or re-create that industry in ways that better support nature without doing harm. In some cases, this might be a tall order. Refuse to create, and terminate those industries that are destructive to nature. In the next few decades, we'll grapple with these issues. It will be profoundly interesting and exciting.

We create many industries to provide convenience. They support ignorance, laziness and indolence, which are not sexy. It's a slippery slope with side effects that kill. When you hear the word 'convenience', run like hell. In the name of convenience, we work to build a world so safe that we can live in a coma. But then, why live at all? **Living your life alert, aware and conscious is sexy.**

Challenges and adversities build you, so seek more and greater challenges. Become stronger. **Standing up for something is sexy. Telling truth to empower is sexy. Making life the 'gold' you treasure is sexy. Standing for protection and care of life, others and nature is sexy.** And sexy never ages, although your body does.

In the name of 'progress' and an easier life, industry drilled holes and dug trenches in the Earth's crust to suck up and unearth buried plant corpses that had turned into coal, oil and gas. Messes of derricks, towers and oil pools litter every continent. Decades later, these places still do not support the growth of plants.

For centuries, the fishing industry overfished the oceans and left one area after another fished out and depleted. In international waters, no renewal programs or catch limits were ever set. By 2048, scientists predict, there will be no fish in the ocean.

In a mere century, a blip in the age of the Earth, our activities have raised the average global temperature by 1.5°C. Experts and researchers estimate that an increase of 0.5 degrees to 2°C, the world may go into climate collapse. Already, we see more extreme temperatures, more species dying off and becoming extinct, more storms and droughts, and more coral reefs killed by increasing acidity, warming ocean temperatures and climate change. We carry on as though there was nothing to be concerned about. Our stewardship of this lovely, fragile, delicate planet that life gave us as a gift sucks.

Governments create crisis after crisis, media focuses on crisis after crisis, and capitalist entrepreneurs cash in on crisis after crisis. We continue to deny that people's activities have consequences to Earth. Banks fund and profit from both sides of every conflict. Health, peace, self-knowledge, education and environment, our most important topics, get too little attention.

We patch up or suppress symptoms but fail to cure anything. After 200,000 years and 100 billion people living here, we still have no clarity on the nature of health, the roots of peace, or the answer to human fulfillment. No wonder we have so many unsolved problems. We're heading rapidly toward the destruction of life and nature. The physicist Stephen Hawking suggests we will be extinct within 1,000 years. Others say that unless we make drastic changes in the way we live, our extinction might happen in this century.

As a part of nature, treat creatures and their sources of support respectfully. As life, value each creature's right to life and to care. As an oxygen-dependent creature, don't burn the air you need to breathe. As a planetary citizen, sow, grow and care for green plants everywhere and get involved in intelligent global water management. In addition, help harness water for energy in ways that also take care of nature and the creatures living here. Be a true human being that supports and nurtures the *home* that supports and nurtures you.

8

BEYOND HEALTH 2:
Infinite Awareness

Wordless

UNION WITH INFINITE AWARENESS, SOMETIMES called the 'BIG picture', is the eighth key part of total sexy health designed by nature. Many words have been used to try to name what cannot be named or known through your senses, but only through awareness of itself. Inadequate words that people use to describe the ultimate reality behind what exists only in experience include: being, perfection, love, infinity and God.

Given that words can't get you there, understand these words as expressions of the experienced reality of that state, not as transporters for you into that experiential reality. Because words cannot take you into wordlessness, you have to leave words behind to enter the pre-word inner realm. This is quite possible. You and every other child came into the world alive and present in that pre-word state. You spent your first (pre-birth) five to nine months in it.

Awareness of the infinite is the most profound experience

possible for human beings. In it, you're one with all that is. It's especially sweet to feel that state of grace as a concept-free experience while you are alive in human form. It is sexier than anything else in the world. In it is safety. Safety is sexy. In it, all things naturally unfold at the perfect pace. That's sexy. From it, all that exists emerges. In it, all that exists has its being. Into it, all that exists dissolves after its natural timespan in physical form is completed.

What's your access to this state of being? The answer should not surprise you, but it might. The emptiness or ache you feel in your chest when you experience being lonely, heart-broken, lost, empty, blue, disappointed or in sorrow is your entry point for coming home to your self. Why? Life uses the pain of your separation from your most basic being, your deepest self, to remind and call you home to the 'ground' of your being.

Do you want to know your essence? Do you want to discover all that's within you? Then be with yourself. Make time for solitude. Sit with that ache. Feel it. Just feel it. It's okay to feel it and to cry. It will not hurt you. Don't judge it, and don't try to understand it with your mind or in words. It is not something you can figure out in your head. Your heart calls your awareness to come home. You can live your life in that fulfilled feeling of home within your being. It transforms your knowledge of who you are and what you feel, which then drives your thinking, leads to your speaking, directs your actions in more life-affirming ways, and leads to better quality-of-life destinations and destinies.

Your direct inner knowing of wholeness heals and transforms your fractured world, from needy and discontent to perfectly fine. You transform from want to have, ask to answer, and seek to find. You move from take to give, hoard to share, and destroy to construct. You change from hold on to let go, doubt to trust, and learn to teach. Nothing except the ache in your chest draws you to inner knowing. Power, money, fame and beliefs all fail you in this regard.

Oneness happens when you accept what is and change your

focus from what's on the surface to what's deeper. It's how you change your world, beginning with experiential, direct knowledge of yourself and your personal world.

Acceptance is not an act of giving up your power. Rather, it is using the power you have to acknowledge what is. This includes self-acceptance, the starting point of your most important journey. To successfully achieve your goal of living in your core experience, show up in the starting blocks. What are the starting blocks? They are your heartache and emptiness, which call you to know wholeness. To improve your experience of life, first acknowledge and accept your need for it. Then you know what to address. This is part of therapies like Alcoholics Anonymous and Narc-Anon. It is also part of wisdom-based teaching traditions of all cultures in every part of the world.

Only after you observe and accept what is can you deepen and broaden awareness, set different clear goals, design necessary frameworks, and take steps that get you from where you are to where you want or need to be. You consistently apply this principle in your business. But it is equally important to consistently apply this principle in your personal lives.

Surrender

The word 'surrender', when used in the context of the inner experience of being is not the same as giving up or admitting defeat like at the end of a war, but more like the simple act of letting go. Let go of the mental structures that define, confine and trap you by setting boundaries and limits to your experience. Let go of all that is not the essence of you. Relinquish the impressions of the world on you, and the surfaces of all things in the world that you perceive with your senses. Release the thoughts, memories and fantasies that you create and cling to in your mind. Axe your addiction to the momentum of incessant activities. Pink-slip your body sensations and the light, sound, feeling and taste within you.

You're left with being aware of being aware, and witnessing

everything as it unfolds within and around you in the
boundlessness you are, without interference.

When you let go of everything that limits you, you eventually
end up with the essence of who you truly are. You can let go of
your impressions of the world, your thoughts, your body and
the energy of life. But, it's impossible to let go of awareness.
When you let go OF something, you also let go TO something.
Beyond pure awareness, there's nothing to let go to. There's just
more awareness. It's who you are and what your essence is. It is
your identity with infinity.

This is not just infinity's existence in you. It is also your
existence in infinity, and being at one with it. It does not exist
in theory. It is only and purely experiential. This is your eternal
home and nature. This is your foundation and your being. This
is what your world, mind, body and life came out of, dwell in
and return to when your journey through the illusion of time
and space is over. This is your ultimate, indivisible, invisible
foundation. It's content-free. It's formless and indestructible.
It's undifferentiated. It's aware. Some people call it 'cosmic
consciousness', but I prefer the more humble 'awareness'
designation.

Within this awareness, you can watch and witness the light
energy—your radiance, life and presence within—swirl and
endlessly unfold.

Within it, you hear a sound like surf waves crashing on a
beach, or the rush at the bottom of a waterfall. It is the sound
you hear when you stop and listen into a deep silent snowy
winter night in the woods in Northern Canada. It seems like
that sound is all around you, but it's the sound of your life
energy filling the reach of awareness of your sense of hearing.

Within this awareness, you feel the fullness of your life
within your inner emptiness, and can taste the sweetness of life
even in the absence of taste within you. You become aware of all
of creation unfolding from this center-point of existence.

From within surrender's stillness, you observe without
mental interference. From there, you can discover everything.

For instance, you'll notice that some foods work better for your body than others, and you'll gravitate toward healthier choices. For example, I found that fresh, unprocessed, whole and mostly plant-based whole foods work best for me. I've also noticed that I have more energy on raw than on cooked foods, and that fried foods lower my energy and make me tired. From the stillness of that surrender, you access the wisdom that guides you to engineer your *perfect sexy life journey.*

Peace

For eons, peace has been a hope of humanity, especially in times of conflict and war, but it's always eluded us and has never been realized. Religions promise peace after death. How cynical! I'm confused now, while I'm alive. I need peace now while I'm alive. To me, it seems unfair to be forced to wait for peace until after death. In truth, peace is possible here and now.

Governments claim to attain peace by appeasement, negotiation or threat. They define peace as the absence of war, which is more accurately called a 'cease-fire'. They've led you to believe that peace comes from deals and agreements with other groups, against low odds that the agreements will be kept and honored. Eventually, discontent people go back on the word they give and agreements they make. Then the sad dance of diplomacy and threat begins again.

True peace has never been clearly defined. Let me do that now. Real peace is present within you as a state of being. Real peace is present within every human being. Peace is an experience rather than a belief or concept. In moments in which you know peace, you know how real it is. In moments in which you don't know it, peace has no reality for you. Then you only have concepts, and concepts about peace are NOT peace.

Peace has roots within you. It is the deepest part of your being. True peace exists in the reality of being and is not real in theory. Peace is internal before it's external, personal before it is social or political, and felt before its power is expressed and acted on.

Let me belabor the point. Peace is *everywhere that's real*. The only place where peace does not exist is in what's NOT real. What's not real? Memories, thoughts, beliefs and fantasies are not real. Peace cannot exist in fantasy, as peace is real, and fantasies are imaginary.

The degree to which we don't feel peace is the degree to which we live in fantasy. We live our lives mostly in fantasy. That's why we miss the peace that's already everywhere present. We know peace when we become real by connecting our awareness to the reality of peace within us. **Real peace is *powerfully sexy*.**

Peace is everywhere, but *only peace perceives peace*. Only peace recognizes peace. Only peace knows peace. If you don't observe peace everywhere, peace in you is not observing. You can't feel, perceive, or experience peace from an inner state of being of non-peace. To know peace, look deeply into your inner silence. There, you'll find that peace completely fills the depth of your solitary being. You discover that the peace in you extends from the core of your being out to infinity. When you find and feel that, you know that peace is everywhere, even in the midst of dissent, conflict and war.

People fighting wars do not look into or from the peace within them. During fighting, they do not focus in the core of their inner being. They focus mentally and physically on an external enemy, with whom they play an unacknowledged but mutually agreed on game of 'I will destroy your body'. If they were aware of their deepest state of being, they'd know that peace fills them, each of their 'enemies' who are not really enemies, all space in between and around them, and all time in its present moment.

In war, both sides ignore the peace that's everywhere, fight each other for trinkets, risk and destroy bodies for material gains or conceptual supremacy, only to lose these trivial trinkets again the moment that their body ends. What exactly is the point of that?

Where exactly is the state of peace that you can know and experience? Let's examine this question. Is peace in the surfaces of things in the ever-changing world that you live in and inhabit? Yes, because peace is everywhere, but your peace does not come from that ever-changing world of surfaces of things. Is peace a property of human minds? In other words, can you think or imagine peace into existence? None can think or imagine peace into existence, because peace is real, but thinking and imagination are arbitrary and transient.

Is peace an attribute of the human body? Peace is everywhere including within your body, but peace is not physical, so focus on the physical will not put you in touch with peace. Is peace an attribute of life? Life is energy that flows and moves. Life is formless light. Life is not peace, although there is peace also in life.

Is peace within awareness? Peace is awareness. When you become inwardly aware of awareness, you become aware of the utter peace that's the core essence of your being and all other beings. Peace witnesses and watches the light of life dance in your inner darkness, hears the sound of life play in your inner silence, feels the feeling of life filling your inner emptiness, and tastes the sweetness of life in your inner void.

Many masters over the ages talked about peace. They said it's feasible for us to live in and from peace within, real and beyond the mind. Masters practiced voluntary solitude. They used some method to become more self-aware in stillness. They calmed senses, mind and body, and immersed their focus of awareness in the core of their inner being. The only difference between them and us is their commitment to practice, and the depth to which they were aware of their internal being. They went deep. **Going deep is sexy**.

Most of us ignore our inner being and spend our time in external pursuits. Masters focus on what they have and are, ecstatic. We focus on what we want, and complain about not having it. They focus awareness on the changeless ground of being. We focus on the changing surfaces of things and exclude inner practice and inner presence to the peace that, in our core, we are.

Peace is within you and within every human being. Focus awareness inwardly to access it. The more you practice, the more deeply you discover peace without a bottom, which is the essence of all that is. You are peace. It feels full, rich and whole. As peace, you're beyond life and death, darkness and light, thoughts and images, and beyond the body and the world of change. Seen from the reality of peace, the catchphrase that 'the only constant in the world is change' is actually not true.

In peace, you find a world in which all people live their lives lit up from within, take their instructions from life, live in harmony with self, others and nature, and help to take care of the basic needs of all.

Without peace as a personal experience, you can't feel whole and cared for. You can't give yourself completely, because you're not fully self-present and are busy trying to get your self taken care of. Then you ignore the fact that you've been, ARE and always will be cared for perfectly by life in peace. Every moment of every day, through all dramas, traumas and changes that take place in the physical, mental, social and natural worlds, peace takes perfect care of you.

Peace is the top experience that you can have. When you feel it, everything else in your life comes together. Cultivate peace when you have time and luxury to do so. If you don't, you'll create mental conflict that leads to physical discord and later to war. I know it from personal experience, both of the war into which I was born and the peace within the depth of my being that I now enjoy. Inner peace is **profoundly sexy**. Should you cultivate peace? That is up to you.

Source

Source is that out of which all things emerge, within which all things exist and into which all things dissolve again after their time in form is done. Source holds everything and everyone in its embrace. Trust it to be all loving, everywhere present, all knowing and all-powerful. Even though your attention is largely focused on taking care of your body, you're not the body. You're not your ideas, concepts or beliefs, either. You're not your family, your tribe or your social and natural environment. In your indestructible, essential being, you're the undifferentiated, infinite awareness within which energy, matter, time and space merge, and from within which they all emerge.

This Source cannot be described, but it is real and can be known. You know it, not by your will or effort, but by your accepting presence. By letting go, you become one with it. In moments in which you feel one with it, your life flows effortlessly within your physical, social and environmental contexts.

This is not wishful thinking, hope for an afterlife based on fear, or a religious theory that 'expert' committees generate or invent from reading old books and exercising intellect and imagination. Knowing your source comes from your personal inner discovery and experience.

You get into that knowing when you move awareness into the inner stillness that you find in voluntary solitude. You come to know your own being when you sit, quiet, long and often enough, with awareness focused in the center of your being. You'll become that experience when life and your body separate at death (more in chapter 12), but profound self-knowledge is also accessible while you live. **Sitting with your longing to know the truth of the deepest origin of your life is sexy.**

Most of you ignore that deep longing and live your life chasing small trinkets that cannot bring you solid satisfaction. You miss the greatest gift you have within you. You miss its awesome magnificence distracted by long series of short-term baubles of passing value. You live in a world that's falling down due to the discontent you feel because you disconnected your awareness from the inner peace that is your source. You distract yourself or blame others and circumstances for that ache you don't like feeling, which resulted from letting your awareness drift away from your source.

Feel that ache. It is the greatest gift you've been given, other than being alive. The ache calls you to bring your awareness back home within to your source. In that return and in that source, you find everything for which you have ever deep down yearned, ached, hoped and prayed. It's always been there for you, in you. Always. Never for a moment has it left you, even in your darkest, most frightening and desperate circumstances and times. You've kept awareness away from your source. Any time, like the prodigal son or daughter, you can initiate the journey home. You'll not be punished or judged when you return to unconditional love. In your heart, you've always been accepted and welcomed, and loved without judgment.

However, you've missed the richness of the full experience of your life in every moment in which your awareness drifted randomly around in the world. You can't gain back the time you lost but you can re-connect and enjoy the time you have left while you have it. When the party's over, the dancers leave the stage, the lights go dark and we all MUST then go home into our self, back to our origin, into the formless knowledge out of which we came.

To live your life, here and now, knowing the infinite and peace embedded in it is the greatest state of being possible for you and every member of humanity. You don't have to wait for anyone else to get there. You can live simultaneously present in all 8 parts: source, life energy, inspiration, body, safety, social ease, nature and the infinite 'field' (calm presence) that permeates them all. **The infinite 'field' is eternally sexy**.

In a life like that, everything works. Do you want this kind of life? Is it something you'll pursue and commit daily time to tap into? Can you get there without help, by yourself, alone? By all means, try. If you want help to take a step or two in that direction, help is available. If you want help, ask. **Asking for help when you know you need it is sexy**. I can point you in the direction of success in this profoundly sacred, sexy undertaking. Ask your heart what it aches for and needs. Sit with that ache. Let it direct you to its balm. So much is possible for you, and the world needs you on this journey into truth and personal power.

Still Real

Brain, mind, and understanding cannot grasp the 'field' because your brain, mind and understanding are far too small and limited to hold, enfold or to encompass it. Having no boundaries, it is so much larger than your personal boundaries that you can know it only when you let go, surrender your little self to it, and merge your smallness in its vastness. Your access to it is through an always-open door in your core, from which it extends boundlessly outward to the infinite, forever, and all-encompassing eternal moment.

Infinite awareness exists, but not in speculations or theories created from imagination. It is so real that you can never grab it academically. You cannot conquer it. You let go into it. When you try to grab, own, steal, create, muscle your way to, confiscate or invent it, you lose your connection to it.

A sage by the name of Kabir once said, regarding how to experience this reality, "All I do is relax, and awareness does my *'stillness practice'* for me." There's nothing to get done here. You can't pull it to you or push it away because you are it. Just notice. It is already in you, as you, as your most basic personal reality. Become alert to awareness. Observe that it has no inner or outer boundaries. It is the insubstantial 'substance' that constructs all that is in the cosmos; an edgeless canister within which all that is appears, floats, dances and disappears again.

While your access to the basic, ultimate reality is inward, once you know it, you notice that it's not confined to just your physical dimensions. It expands forever outward, and you've always been at the center of it. You've always been one with its infinity. So has always every human being been. This indefinable reality is like a sphere with infinite centers and no surface.

It's no wonder that, using their mind, scientists have been unable to get a handle on and comprehend it. Mind and measurement work in duality, defining what it is and telling it apart from what it's not. You can't get to the 'unified field' by schemes and numbers. It's actually quite funny. Genius scientists can't nail it down, but newborn babies with no words or education are one with it. A jellyfish with no brain at all lives in it. You ARE, in your deepest and most basic nature, the 'unified field' that Einstein searched for and never got a handle on. Ultimate reality can't exist as an abstract mathematical formula. Too real for that, it exists only as its self, your self, your being, your non-verbal, non-formula knowing and your peace, where only knowingness itself can be.

This is the peace that is already everywhere, that only peace in you can know, and that you can only know because you are that peace. In the foundation of peace, the universe unfolds. In peace, a flower blooms. In peace, you breathe. In peace, you think. In peace, your vocal cords make sounds that you can recognize as words. In peace, you act. In peace, the consequences of your acts show up. In peace, you reach your goals and destinations. In peace, you age and die. Without this peace, nothing at all is even possible.

It is the deep reality in which all people and all creatures live. In this reality, mountains rise and erode, Earth turns, stars explode, the sun shines, water flows downhill, green things grow, and you manifest thoughts into forms. In this reality, all things, both good and bad, take place. In this reality, the good wolf and the bad wolf in you fight. The one you feed will win. What do you feed them? You feed them observation and attention. What gets attention grows.

When we punish the bad wolf in us, it grows, because it gets attention. Only by feeding the good wolf can we starve the bad wolf. All this takes place within our sphere of influence and infinite awareness. How you focus that awareness, and what you focus on creates your world and universe. What do you want to grow? Attend to that. It is our power and freedom, as well as our responsibility.

Beyond Again

Infinite awareness is beyond life and death. It is beyond time and space, beyond energy and matter, beyond light and darkness, beyond sound and silence, beyond feeling and emptiness. Infinite awareness is beyond inner and outer. In fact, we cannot picture it at all. It's a sphere that has no inside or outside. It has centers everywhere (every human being and all points in space are its centers), but no outside boundaries. It is in every 'here', but in no 'there'. It is in every 'now', but not in any 'then'.

As infinite awareness, you are formless infinite potential, within which everything unfolds perfectly. As life, you are one manifestation of undifferentiated oneness and its infinite possibilities. As a body designed and constructed by life, you can act in the interests of safety and thriving for all. As inspired mind, you can design almost unlimited applications for physical comfort and safety. As social being, you can connect, share and cooperate with other members of your group, to be better together. As part of nature, you can take and use resources, and become a resource for others.

As a being whose nature is, all at the same time, infinite awareness, sunlight energy, an inspired mind, physical matter, survival smarts, a member of social groups and a part of planetary nature, you are rich and full beyond belief, and anything is possible for you. Fully present in all of your being, you live like a master who lights up the world s/he lives in.

This is an option for each of the 8 billion citizens who live here now. This was the potential of each one of 100 billion people who graced (or disgraced) this planet in the past 200,000 years of human existence. How many people in those years and of those numbers have lived fully present in all of their being? No one knows, because full mastery of presence was not on any census ever done, and not everyone who mastered living fully present attracted public or widespread attention. Full presence is a personal matter that may or may not be shared widely in history or written literature.

When you listen to how discontent people are, how easily they fly off the handle, and how much they gripe and play victim, you can conclude that living fully present to the depths of all of our magnificent being is still rare. Every human being COULD live like that because it is built in and comes standard with being human, but few have found their way back to their own fullness. Most people have lived far below what's possible for them because their stories obscured their potential. That appears to have been as true in the past as it is today.

What about you? Can you live simultaneously present in the physical, mental, social and natural world and with what is beyond the visible, the physical and the imagined? Can you live life in the full reality of all of your being? Let me be clear. **You CAN!! But do you want to?**

Is it worth commitment, time and effort to live fully conscious and aligned with all of what your nature is? Don't give me an answer to that question. I don't need to know. It is a question you can ask and answer for yourself. You cannot answer it in words. You answer it in your presence. You answer it in how you fill this moment. You answer it within each 'NOW' of your existence. You answer it in where your focus goes.

Within your world of appearances, social contracts, ways of acting, speaking, thinking and feeling, beyond learned and unexamined habits and beyond your chores and routines is your deeper true reality. It calls to your heart to come home and find the 'I AM' within your being.

You are the peace you ache for in your times of loss, pain, shame and grief. Endless gifts await you. Come home. Unpack each gift. You're welcome here, and you are home and cherished here. You're unconditionally loved, and you are whole and perfect here. Only here, within, will you find all you've deep down always yearned for, and have never found out there in the world of surfaces. YOU are what you always longed, searched, prayed and hoped for. **Hacking and unpacking the gift you are is sexy**.

Life and breath can save you. In stillness, you find your deeply rich prosperity. In quiet voluntary solitude, you find an end to your distractions and embrace the power and the glory of reality.

9

EMOTIONAL HEALTH:
Composite

Definition

HAVING DESCRIBED THE EIGHT PARTS of total sexy health designed by nature, let us consider emotions. They're complex composites of these eight key parts.

Because of their complexity, even those who work with emotions on a daily basis in the practice of psychology and psychiatry find them difficult to define. Studying the subject, I found no experts whose clarity on the subject impressed me. A few years ago, I read a definition of emotions in *The Power Of Now* by Eckhart Tolle, who is not a psychologist. "Emotion," he wrote, "is your body's response to your thoughts."

That simple sentence triggered a cascade of insights that led to how I presently view the nature of emotions. The fact that they get input from each of the eight parts of nature and human nature makes emotions complicated. Here is a preliminary definition. Maybe you can improve on it.

In response to thoughts triggered by how you perceive and interpret events, you generate EMOTIONS that harness life

energy to enhance physical expressions and actions to more forcefully push or pull you in the direction of goals you've set in your mind in the hope that you'll feel better when you attain them.

Here is a slightly longer version. It might help you (or not).

In response to (**changing**) thoughts triggered by your perception and (**memory- and imagination-informed**) interpretation of (**inner and outer**) (**changing**) events (**people, situations, circumstances**), you generate (**changing**) EMOTIONS that harness (**your**) life energy (**more powerfully**) to enhance (**your**) (**different**) physical expressions and actions to more forcefully push (**against resistance, interference or failure**) or pull you (**toward a personally defined outcome**) in the direction of (**personal or group**) goals you've set in your mind in the (**conscious or subconscious**) hope that you'll feel better (**proud, powerful, satisfied, content, cared for, whole, loved, etc.**) when you attain them.

This definition of emotions is complex, because all eight parts of nature and human nature contribute to them on a moment-to-moment basis. Not only are emotions complex, but also they're idiopathic, uniquely personal, and constantly changing. You often find it difficult to 'get' other people's emotions because you don't live in their shoes. You don't know have the same individual wiring that underlies, supports and determines the stories and personal meaning people give to emerging events. Other people's responses can be so different from yours that you don't understand how anyone can be so emotional about something or someone that stirs nothing in you.

Standing side by side in a situation, one person may go ballistic about what s/he sees, hears, and feels, and may have an intense outburst, while the other person remains completely detached and cool, and watches the same situation unfold with profound indifference. Objectively, it's the same situation for both. Subjectively, what goes on in the mind and body of these two people is drastically different. Clearly, the difference is not in the situation, but in what each person brings to it.

All people bring an abundance of contributing factors to every situation. They result from individual personal histories. They're stored memories, interpretations and meanings given to the sequences of events and people in their lives, which program their nervous system-computer. Did they perceive the world and people to be unfriendly or friendly? How did they experience, and what meaning did they give to their life events. How did they deal with the events? What did they learn in the process?

This is how human nervous networks develop and connect, creating unique (idiopathic) personalities and personal ways of responding to situations in the course of living. Wise teachers suggest that we not judge people until we've walked a mile in their moccasins. We'll return to this topic later.

Composite

Let's examine what each of the eight parts of nature and human nature contributes to emotions.

1.   **Internal Awareness**: This still point exists within the core of your being. When you're aware of the stillness in your being, you feel calm and present. You feel confident in that calm presence. You feel powerful and capable. **Stillness, calm presence, power, and competence are sexy.**

People trust you without knowing why they trust you. Why do they trust you? In this, your deepest state of being, you embody and radiate the wholeness that is also their deepest state of being. **Reflecting their wholeness back to others by being in it is sexy.**

They want to spend time with you because you don't lean on them when you know how to lean into your self. That's sexy, too. If you're not aware of that stillness, you're more likely to be skittish, agitated and pushy. This is not so sexy. People then do not find you nearly as attractive as when you're naturally cool because you connect to your natural inner cool stability.

Your level of internal awareness influences what emotions you bring to any situation.

2. **Life Energy**: Your awareness connected with that energy, you shine and radiate a presence that exudes personal power, vitality and lightness. **Energy, vitality and lightness are attractive and sexy.** People trust lit up people because they trust the light that is life. They want to be in touch with that light, and if they're not, they'll gravitate to the light in you.

If you're not aware of living lit up from within, you'll be darker in your feelings, thoughts, words and actions. You're likely less fun to be around, more moody, more annoying in your verbal expressions and more heavily destructive in your behavior. That's will repel people, who'll keep more distance from you.

Your connectedness to life energy influences what emotions you bring to any situation.

3. **Inspired Creative Mind**: Creative people are fun to be with. They think out of the box and are not stuck in a rut. **Originality is sexy.** You idolize composers, authors, musicians, singers, painters, sculptors, dancers, acrobats, inventors, designers and poets. They're turned on and turn you on. **The act of creation is sexy.** They see options. **Seeing options is sexy.**

With loss of creativity, you lose inspiration and hope, get down in your mood and then develop a victim mentality. Then sexy leaves the building. We want to help depressed victims. **Helping is sexy**, but depressed is not.

Your level of inspired creativity influences what emotions you bring into any situation.

4. <u>Physical Body</u>: **A fit, active body kept healthy by eating and drinking in line with nature is sexy.** It exudes confidence, strength, and competence. A sick and unfit body is neither attractive nor sexy.

Your physical health and fitness levels, which depend on what was described in Chapter 4, influence what emotions you bring to any situation.

5. <u>Survival Smarts</u>: Protection and safety are important issues, and you admire those who confidently deal with crises, save bodies from danger, put out fires, patch up injuries and give generously to the needy. **Protection and safety are sexy.** Not being able to deal with emerging situations is not sexy.

Your level of survival competence influences what emotions you bring to any situation.

6. <u>Social Group</u>: **Feeling relaxed and easy with others, and connecting and communicating well are sexy.** People who act well on teams are sexy. **A good sense of humor is sexy.** People who encourage others are sexy. People who are socially stiff and uncomfortable are not so sexy.

Your social ease or its lack influences what emotions you bring to any social context or situation.

7. <u>Natural Environment</u>: **Being natural and comfortable in nature is sexy.** People who admire, respect and appreciate nature are sexy. People who are comfortable naked are sexy. People who enjoy their senses are sexy. People who respond elegantly to the

pleasures of touch are sexy. People who fear nature or their nature are not sexy.

Your relationship with nature and your nature influences what emotions you contribute to any situation.

8. <u>**Infinite Awareness**</u>: This is the still field of vastness in which you live. People who are one with and trust the infinite awareness that includes everything are sexy. Feeling cared for in the knowledge that we live and die, they accept, protect, care for, appreciate and help others with calmness, confidence and equanimity. They're not afraid of competition because they know that there's room for all in a universe that takes care of all things and creatures in the most profoundly beautiful internal and interrelated way, no matter what their journey is and where they are on that journey. **Being at ease with the BIG picture is sexy**.

People who don't trust the way the universe unfolds tend to be anxious and fearful, which is not sexy. They fear to include others because it's a 'dog eat dog' world from which they must hide or with which they must fight. This kind of person is much less sexy.

Your level of comfort with the BIG PICTURE influences what emotional state you bring to any situation.

Unique

Emotions develop under historical, experiential, sequential, linguistic, idiopathic, and interactive influences in each individual.

- **The development of each person's unique emotional makeup**

- **Begins at conception**
- **Involves**
  - ◻ **The precise succession of contexts, circumstances, situations, events and people**
  - ◻ **Incessant, persistent, intense and complicated interactions between person and world**
  - ◻ **Perceptions, interpretations and meanings the person creates from these and**

- **Results in specific neural connections and pathways that constitute the person's unique personality**

Settings, time sequences, succession of events, perceptions, creative interpretations, memories, expectations and anticipations all contribute to how exactly this wiring of brain, mind and body takes place to create your emotional makeup, and the background that you bring to and impose on situations in the present.

Recent research has shown that, shockingly, 90% of the content of eyewitness reports of events is internally sourced mental input provided by her/his wiring, imagination and memory. This unrelated mental input may even contradict the actual event that's taking place, which is ostensibly being reported objectively. On verification, merely 10% of eyewitness reports turn out to be correct details of what truly occurred. Oy!

Like all human beings, you bring lots of stuff from your vast collection of life events and experiences into your observation of your every present situation. You add a great deal of extraneous, personal, non-objective information to your observations & interpretations of what happens, and this strongly influences how you respond or react. We all do.

This explains why and how so much miscommunication occurs between human beings. You think of your memories, observations, interpretations and beliefs as truth. Everyone else thinks that his/her mental makeup is truth. In fact, they/re all just stories we create, hold and carry. Nothing we think is true or objective. No thought is real. Our thoughts are subjective, personal, slanted and both hopelessly biased and irrational.

When you acknowledge the subjective, personal nature of your emotions, you begin to better understand how important it is to learn to step out of your mental makeup, see situations from the perspective of pure awareness, and address them in ways that, freed from your personal, prejudicial, perceptual bias, lead to better outcomes for all involved.

Is this possible? It requires you to cultivate pure awareness beyond the personal biases of memory, belief and imagination, and use your senses to see, hear and feel what is happening while minimizing your distorting mental filters. Imagine the kind of world you can build if you know how to put the basket of biases in your head aside. Imagine the kind of world that the ability of all citizens to put their mental biases aside could create.

What are your biases? You learned biases from stories your parents told you. You bias your children with stories about your identity by blood and family history. Your concepts, stories, ideas and beliefs, carry biases about race, gender, culture, politics, religion and money. You carry personal experience biases. You carry negative biases founded on discontent. You carry ignorance biases, too. These biases serve many agendas against benefiting all at the expense of none, and they ultimately work against your benefit, too. **Being aware of your biases is sexy**.

You're much more than your institutions expect you to be. The more of your true and bias-free self you discover and become, the less you insert biases into your perception, and the less you depend on these biases and the agendas they promote. The less you depend on these, the freer you are to create fresh agendas for the good of all.

What are the agendas of institutions? There are only a few. Most institutions begin with the purpose of protecting and serving their members. With time, the focus gradually shifts to self-preservation. Still later, institutional focus may morph to maintaining power and control.

Many of our major institutions, especially governments, now work for the bank more than they work to administer the affairs of the citizens they were created to serve. This includes institutions in all sectors: villages, towns, cities, provinces, states, regions and countries, as well as various religious factions and denominations, and others.

Self-knowledge frees you. The more satisfaction you get from the richness of the feeling of life within you, the less you depend for it on outside influences and influencers. Then you can rein in the excesses of institutions simply by voting with your wallet. If you lack self-fulfilling self-knowledge, you seek to get satisfied by endless distractions or through never-ending consumption of external goods and services, which ultimately fail you and damage your social and natural surroundings.

Progress

Your emotions serve as personal assessment/measure of your progress toward the attainment of goals you have set for yourself.

Negative emotions express your assessment that progress toward your goals is being thwarted, and you direct your negative emotions against the people and situations that you perceive, interpret and assess as 'getting in your way' and blocking or interfering with what you want. These are your 'upset' emotions.

You generate anger at situations or people and fight or bully them if you think you can win that way. You generate fear or victimize yourself if you believe they will defeat you. You become devious if you think you can sneak your way to your goals without being noticed and stopped.

Embarrassment is your self-assessment of not being enough in social situations. Guilt and shame are self-assessments of falling short regarding your behavior according to the rules imposed on you by others. Hopelessness and despair result from not seeing a way forward past what you perceive is blocking you. A reprimand consists of negative emotions and words that you impose on underlings when they don't act as you wish or command them to act to take you closer to your goals. You can look at the other negative emotions like heartache, blues, anxiety and depression, and figure out for yourself what they assess. You can do this generally concerning social groups, and you can also do it specifically with regards to your own life and personal goals.

Positive emotions express your assessment of satisfaction with your progress toward your goals. They're your celebratory 'success' emotions. Gratitude is acknowledgement that what you're focusing on is going really well. Relief is the emotion that you make yourself feel when you've overcome an obstacle on the path to your goal.

Exuberance, joy and a fist pump accompanied by a yell express that you've scored. Satisfaction is the emotion you feel when your path is clear, and you're moving forward toward your goal. Praise is an emotion you bestow on underlings when they do what you want them to do to move you forward toward your goals. You can look at other positive emotions and determine what they measure, both generally and specifically.

Being aware of and not denying your emotions, positive or negative, is sexy.

Behavior is complicated, and it's often a challenge to know why a person behaves in the way s/he does. Here's one way to better understand behavior.

First, all behavior is goal-oriented. If you have no goal, you're not moved to do anything. Why make an effort to do anything if there's no goal, outcome, result or payoff? Let me illustrate.

A newborn baby has not yet set physical goals. It lies on its back, and its arms and legs flail randomly through the air. It's not trying to stand up. It's not trying to walk. It's not trying to roll over. It's not trying to sit up. It's not trying anything. A baby's activity goals begin a bit later, with more maturity.

You, too, are like that. When there's nothing to do, you might just stay in bed late, and get some extra do-nothing rest. Depressed and hopeless people who lose sight of their goals and don't know how to go forward may stay in bed all day. I know this from past personal and family history.

Second, if you don't understand someone's behavior, ask yourself, "What would have to be the goal of this behavior for it to make sense?" More often than not, when you know a people's goals, their behavior does make sense. Other people's behavior isn't likely to make sense when you try to interpret it in terms of your own goals rather than theirs.

'Irrational' behavior is rational in terms of the goal it serves. This is true, no matter what the focus is: politics, education, family, workplace, addiction, neurosis and crime.

State

When all aspects of health have been taken care of, and you live in alignment with each of the eight parts of nature and your nature, you experience calmness and presence as your dominant emotion. Werner Erhard calls it 'serene passion' and Abraham Maslow, self-actualization'. I call it 'calm presence'.

With calm presence, serene passion and self-actualization come other virtues, including relaxation, care, a sense of fair play, broad perspective, confidence, humor, humility and readiness to do what needs to be done.

Emotions express, in a goal-oriented fashion, the exact way in which one (or more) of the eight parts of nature and your human nature is in or out of alignment with its nature and function. Each emotion and the actions it motivates is your attempt to get (back) to wholeness.

Since you don't know what exactly you need to do to live in the state of alignment of all eight parts of nature and your nature, you don't often experience serene passion or calm presence, and a lot of what you do is experimental. By trial and error, you find out how things work. If what you do does not get you closer, you try something else.

With time and luck, you may find your way to calm presence, but you may do better if you get help from someone who knows the road you're on and the destination you're stumbling toward. That's why life creates teachers, coaches, mentors and masters. Ask for and accept their help (more on this in Chapter 13).

The goal is not to do it on your own without help. The goal is not to be a proud Lone Ranger. The goal is to get to the goal. The goal is to live fully present in all of your being and nature and to enjoy the time you have being human on Earth. Billions have lived and died without mastering their greatest gift and asset. You'll hinder successful goal attainment if you

- Don't know your goal
- Don't know your starting point
- Don't know the direction in which you need to go
- Are too proud to ask for and accept help, assistance or coaching

Question: Why does it take 100 million sperms to fertilize one egg? Answer: Men just will not stop to ask for directions. Funny? Cracks me up.

Before you race out in ignorance and get yourself trampled, know where you want to go (destination, finish line), where you are right now (origin, starting point), and the path you need to take from origin to destination. It's a requirement for success in all journeys external and internal. We know it regarding external journeys and businesses. We need to apply the same criteria and logic to our internal journey toward full presence in our magnificent self.

Each emotion generates a coherently integrated state of being. Strong emotions feel good. You feel coherent in them. That's true for both positive and negative states of being. Some people get addicted to anger, for instance, because its coherent nature makes them feel personally powerful and focused. **Strong emotions are sexy**.

Anger works for individual, physical, short-term survival. Long-term, it's self-destructive. It burns you out. Also, you know that your body will not ultimately survive, so you might as well give up on survival and focus on thriving. You have a better quality of life when you chase carrots (feel inspired and thrive) than when you run from whips and sticks (manage crises).

Like anger, inner peace is a coherent state of being. Feeling a peace that extends from here in the core of your being out to infinity is more coherently powerful than anger. It is not limited to individual, physical, short-term survival. Peace is alignment with all that is, in the deepest, most extensive timeless way. It's a deeply satisfying, boundless, eternal experience of the cherished state. In peace, you still attend to your physical and social needs but without the stress, pain and burnout of anger. Peace is stress-free. Studies show that it reverses aging.

Thousands of different states of being exist. Each expresses a different emotion. All of them marshal your physical, mental, social and natural resources into a coherent whole. Awareness informs each of them. Each of them focuses you on a goal.

The most powerful state of being for any human, and the one most conducive to living lit up from within, in harmony with others, and getting the needs of all of us met, is the one that living masters embody, teach and encourage. Make it your main goal to remember to be fully present in all of your being as much and as deeply as possible.

State Change

Contrary to the popular notion that you 'can't help it' when you go into a rage or some other state of being that expresses a strong emotion that you feel in the moment, you CAN and do change your states of being instantly and at will. You may not notice the rapid inner process by which you do it, but that doesn't mean that you're not in control of or responsible for it. If you're not responsible for what happens within you, then who is?

When you're fully present into the depths of your life, you can watch yourself generating different states of being and changing your states of being in response to changing people and situations. You're not a victim of your emotions and the states of being you organize around them. In truth, you create each emotion and state of being. I'll give you an example from my past.

One day, my ex-wife and I were having a heated argument that had been going on for more than 30 minutes. We were really going at it, equally hot under our collars. Neither side was de-escalating. Then the phone rang.

Since I was closer to the phone than she, I picked it up, and in a calm, sweet voice said, "Hello." A 5-minute cordial conversation took place on the phone between the caller and me. I giggled at something the other person said. Then we said a calm goodbye, and I gently hung up the phone. Instantly, I resumed my heated argument mode, and my then wife went at it for another 20 minutes.

I had instantly switched my state of being twice in less than 10 minutes. At the time, I said to people that I 'could not help my anger' because my wife made me angry. Many years later, Tony Robbins did an exercise about this topic with 2,000 people in one of his 'Date With Destiny' events. During that exercise, I remembered the incident. There was no way that I could deny that I was in control of my emotions. He asked us, "How fast can you change your state?" His answer (that I now agree with) is, "In a heartbeat!!"

You can instantly change your state in response to external input, or you can break out of it through a moment of 'fierce determination' from within.

You can change your state of being at will. Do you know the power and freedom it gives you? You can choose and change the state of being that you live in. Pick the best one, which is the one in which you and others thrive the most. Live in it.

When something causes you to forget and lose that state for a lesser one and you become aware of it, deliberately pick your cherished state of being again. How do you do that?

Three easy ways of doing it include

1. Stand up straight or sit straight. Good posture puts you into a much better state of being than slouching or collapsing over your chest

2. Consciously breathe into your heart. Bring awareness down from above (heads), and up from below (tails) to the middle of your chest. Breathe into your chest. In the core of being are no words. There IS a feeling of wholeness and presence. Focus in your core. It makes you slightly less tall than when you're focused in your head, but you feel much more centered and wiser.

    In that place of no thoughts, you are who you are. You feel without judgment. From that place, you're free to choose how to feel, what to think and say, where to go and what to do.

3. Focus on the lightness of the light, sound and feeling of life that you are, rather than on the heaviness of your body. Energy is light by nature. It holds your heavy body up. Without it, your body would collapse on the floor, pulled down by gravity. Energy uplifts your body, and also puts you in touch with the power you are.

In your awareness of natural posture, breath and energy, you feel completely cared for. From there, you can invent a purpose for your life. Make it global. Thinking big takes the same energy as thinking small. Cared for by life and feeling it, wanting to care for other people and nature is normal. You can do it in a thousand ways. Pick something that the world needs, you have a passion for, which uses your background, experience, talents, interests and abilities, and that saves others from the drama, trauma, nightmares and pain that you've endured. Ask yourself, "What's the biggest splash for good I can make in one lifetime with one body?" Make it real it in YOUR life first; then, it's easy to bring it to the rest of the world.

Here is mine, one more time.

1. **8 billion people live life lit up from within, because the light is already within each of us, and we now look into it instead of looking away from it.**

2. **In that light, we feel so cared for by life that we don't feel any need to steal other people's stuff, and so we live in harmony together.**

3. **Cared for and in harmony, we share what we don't need with those who need it, and all the basic needs of all are met.**

No one has to sacrifice anything to attain this goal.

Why do people hold on to what they don't even need? Feeling discontent as a result of living disconnected from awareness of life, light, heart and core, they fear that giving away what they don't even need will make them feel even more discontent. As soon as they feel cared for and their discontent dissolves, they can let go of and give what they have no need for to those who need it. Easy peasy, just like that.

10

INTEGRATION:
Seamless

Challenge

THE CHALLENGE OF INTEGRATING 8 parts, each of which has a different nature and function is daunting, but 4.3 billion years of innovation by the boundless genius of the anything-is-possible universe produced a profoundly remarkable integration. In nature, what didn't work was discarded and recycled. Everything that worked was kept and improved on. The fact that you live today proves that you are heir to an unbroken line of reproductive successes that extends back more than 4 billion years. Is it a worthy legacy? It's really impressive. Revere, celebrate and be humbled by it.

The outcome of all this time, and nature's intelligence, has made you so well integrated that you think you're just one thing, when in fact, you're a composite of many, each with distinct properties, attributes and functions, each sexy in its own right, and all of them together way beyond sexy in how sexy they are and how sexy they make you. **You are seamlessly sexy.**

To contemplate this integration leaves you in awe. The limitless exists within the limited, and the limited unfolds within the limitless. The infinite supports the temporary. Sunlight energy dances along chains of molecules, hides in bonds between atoms and waits for release. Set free, it powers activity on all levels from electrons, atoms and molecules to nerve impulse transmission, to heartbeat, to walking and team sports, and to dynamic, living nature.

Thoughts, which are not real, direct life and body into the creation of something that IS real. Words, which are without substance, can lead to cooperation in groups that leads to successful projects of massive proportions, like cities, roads, moon landings, planes and global communication, to name just a few.

Nature, your foundation and the source of your physical resources and body building materials, provides the context in which you live and have your being. All these turned out from an infinite foundation that is made, not of matter, nor of energy, nor even of mind but of pure, formless, undifferentiated awareness that exists within and around everything in all directions. **Total integration is totally sexy.**

You, as a physical entity, did not author these challenges, nor do you control them. You only control the focus of your awareness, which determines what you experience. You couldn't create this integrated wholeness, its ingenious designs, or its endless diversity. You couldn't have invented it through your creative mental design or deliberate action. Awareness and life orchestrate the integration you are within the ground of being. You are the fortunate, undeservingly blessed beneficiary of magnificence, grandeur and beauty so far beyond your comprehension that the best you can do is appreciate and admire them with your jaw hanging open in wonder and awe. **Integrated wholeness, endless diversity and ingenious design are sexy.**

Synergy

In the integration that you are, each part relies on all the other parts. They work as a team. For you to live, no part can function by itself without all of the other parts also playing their role. If any part went missing, you would not exist. Being human depends on every one of the eight different parts of nature and human nature performing its natural act during the short, sweet time you spend alive.

Synergy is the interaction or cooperation of two or more organizations, substances or other agents to produce combined effects greater than the sum of their separate effects. That's a nice definition, but the synergy that defines you goes far beyond this, and if you look at each of the eight parts of nature and human nature, you find synergies in every part as well as synergies between and beyond the different parts. **Synergy is sexy**.

The synergistic interactions produce such coherent coordination of functions that the parts seem inseparable and the differences between them become invisible. For the sake of greater appreciation, let's separate and make them visible.

Imagine yourself without awareness or without life. Don't imagine it. Look at a creature without awareness and life, like road kill, a skeleton, the 'catch' of a fisherman or hunter, or a corpse. Synergy.

Imagine yourself without creative mind. You'd be alive, but you'd be like a tree, a shrub, a flower or a blade of grass, unable to dream, imagine, hope or feel inspired. Synergy.

Imagine yourself without a body, without activity, without food, water or air. You'd be looking at angels who might be conscious, but incapable of carrying out any of your cherished physical activities. Synergy.

Imagine yourself without survival mind. You would be senseless (blind, deaf, dumb and numb) and the next hungry carnivore that comes along would eat your body. Synergy.

Imagine yourself without other human beings. You would not last long. You survive and thrive because you learned to communicate, specialize your skills and work together for the good of all. Alone, you can't run as fast, scratch as deeply, bite as deadly, jump as high, climb as effectively, fight as hard or fly as high as many other creatures. You could not reproduce alone. Social networks and division of labor made it possible for you to thrive. Synergy.

Imagine yourself without nature's resources. You'd have no sunshine air, water or food. Without gravity, you'd just float up and away into the cold dark death of space. You'd have no body and no materials for clothes and shelter. You'd have no industry and no conveniences. You would not exist. Synergy.

Without awareness and the peace that fills the universe, the stress of constant change would kill you. Within the constant change, the changeless is available to you, and you can rest in it. Synergy.

The whole is greater than the sum of its parts. Being fully present in all parts of nature and your nature creates for you the knowledge and experience of synergy that makes you infinitely sexy and attractive.

Automatic

What's cool about integration is that there's nothing that you can or must do to make it happen. Imagine the job you'd have if you had to consciously do every action that life generates in your body naturally, including breathe, digest, metabolize, circulate blood, beat heart, conduct nerve impulses, contract muscles, filter kidney, move bowels, detox liver and repair injuries.

Life automates for you almost everything in your body. Awareness that is not beheld by you uses energy of which you're not normally conscious, to run the show. The ability to think allows you to create, but the basics are and always were on automatic.

Nature provides light, oxygen, water and foods containing nutrients, fiber, probiotics and enzymes for body repair and construction. Your senses alert you to danger and threat, as well as to care and opportunity. The groups to which you belong help you with skills. You get to decide some of your thoughts and physical activities but almost everything else is outside your conscious control.

You seem to have choice over your feelings, thoughts, words and actions, but some experts say only 2% of your thoughts are conscious, and 99.9% of everything that goes on within your body is beyond your awareness. You notice some of it, but you generate almost nothing of what goes on in nature and the universe. Automatically, life takes care of you when you love and cherish it, and also when you ignore, hate, curse or abuse it.

You can choose to move your awareness from place to place within your being and the world within which you live, but you create none of it. You have limited freedom. Where you focus awareness defines your reality.

Focus awareness on

- The infinite, and you get to know infinity
- Nature, and you come to know nature
- Your group, and you become adept at social interaction
- Survival, and you become adept at protection and reproduction
- Food and fitness, and you improve physical health and performance
- Creativity, and you become an artist or creator
- Life, and you elevate yourself and feel more energetic
- Awareness, you become the witness of all that is as it unfolds

Which one of these are you? You're each of them, and all of them together. You're infinite inner awareness, life, inspiration, body, performance, thoughts, group member, child of nature and infinite awareness.

Imagine seeing yourself as all of these. With practice, it's possible. Just as, with daily practice, you've become good at eating breakfast, dressing, showering and hitting the sack, practicing self-awareness every day makes you good at living a life that feels full, whole, rich and amazingly sexy. Each moment, you can choose where you park your awareness and what you focus on. And yet, almost everything remains, lucky for you, integrated and automatic. Your job: You get to enjoy it all!!

Integrity

Without integration, integrity is not possible. Without integrity, nothing works. Aligning awareness with and giving each part of nature and human nature its due, you optimize integration, and super-sexy integrity results. Integrity means all parts are present, each functioning according to its nature, and all parts including the powerful core of your being, your clearly directed mental focus, and your body in action work together toward goals, outcomes, destinations and destinies in the social and natural world that maintain or re-establish the harmony of wholeness.

Integrity means that you are who you say you are, and do what you say you'll do. **Integrity that embodies honest, forthright standards is sexy**.

When you live disconnected from parts of your being, you feel discontent. When you feel discontent, you live out of line with your own integrity. Out of line with integrity, you lie, cheat, steal, kill, deceive, embezzle and commit crimes: ineffective attempts to heal the discontent that comes from living out of line with your nature. The cure is to simply get back into alignment with the nature of your nature, back to integrity.

Let's examine what integrity is like, regarding each of the eight parts of health based in nature and human nature.

1. **'Internal' awareness integrity**: Internal awareness can never be out of integrity, but you may not be

focused on it, in which case you don't know its integrity. As soon as you bring your awareness back in touch with internal awareness (you are now aware of being aware), you're back to feeling the integrity that is the core of your being. Try it. Sit still alone. Close your eyes. Become aware of being aware. Experience it. Know it. Be that awareness. It is the foundation of integrity in your feelings, thoughts, words and actions. You are that awareness and that integrity.

2. **Life energy integrity**: Life energy can never be out of integrity, but your awareness may not be focused on it, in which case you do not know its integrity. As soon as you bring your awareness back in touch with the sexy light, sound and feeling of the energy that is your life, you're back in the integrity of the energy you are. Try it. Sit still, alone. Close your eyes. Become aware of the light in your inner darkness, the sound in your inner silence, and the calm within your inner restlessness. Be with them. Know them. Identify with them. Be these. Their integration shows up as integrity in feeling, thought, word and action. You are that light, sound and feeling and you are that integrity.

3. **Inspired/creative mind integrity**: When you lose touch with inspiration and creativity, you lose hope. Then you lose everything. Cultivating creativity and inspiration keeps you positive, growing and making things better. "If you're not busy being born, you're busy dying," said Bob Dylan. Through sexy creativity, you inspire, uplift and improve the sexy quality of people's lives.

4. **Physical body integrity**: Inactivity leads to body breakdown, disintegration. Lack of sunshine,

polluted air and water, lack of essential nutrients, too many poisons and poor digestion interfere with body construction and repair. Living active and in line with nature restores sexy physical integrity.

5. **Survival mind integrity:** Whining and hiding when the going gets tough is not sexy. Integrity is being present in the power of being, confidently addressing emergencies and crises with clarity, and caring and creating safety for self and others.

6. **Social group integrity:** Social fears and discomfort lead to behaviors out of line with integrity. Tell truth in the face of opposition with courage and composure, and powerfully contribute to the good of the group. That is social integrity.

7. **Planetary nature integrity:** Disrespect and fear of nature lead to behavior that's out of integrity and destructive. Respect and gratitude for nature's gifts and resources has **integrity that results in sustainability**.

8. **'Infinite' awareness integrity:** Infinite awareness can never be out of integrity but you may not experience being expanded into it, in which case you don't know it. When you become aware of its infinite extension, integrity extends endlessly out from the core of your being. Try it. Sit still alone, eyes closed. Bring awareness to your core. Extend awareness out. Experience it. Know it. Be it. It's the integrity that shows up as trust in the big picture. You're that awareness and integrity.

Emotional integrity. When you live NOT aligned with any one or more the above eight parts of nature and human nature, your emotions rollercoaster you. Aligned with all eight parts, you live in the emotional integrity of calm presence, free of trivialities and distractions, focused on serving and enjoying life, body, others and nature with your gifts and talents.

Without integrity, nothing works. In integrity, everything is possible, and all parts of your life and world fall into place.

Vision

When every part of you is in integrity, aligned with its nature, clear vision comes to you with ease. When all aspects of nature and your nature are coherent, you manifest a coherent life, speak coherent words, carry out coherent actions, and from these build coherent worlds. From coherence, anything worthwhile becomes achievable.

In addition, when you know fully how perfectly you are being cared for, there's only one task left to do. Help wherever help is needed. This is the foundation of a life of service. **Service is sexy.**

Life gave you a planet to enjoy and do something with. What will you do with it? What do you have talent for? What have you experienced? What do you know? What obsesses you? What pain, lack or loss do you want to eradicate? What is your passion? What do you love? What do you have affinity for? What's the greatest good that you can do with one body in one lifetime?

It's not difficult to identify the problems we've created on this planet. Poverty, greed, war, pollution and environmental destruction are some of the most obvious ones. Each of these problems begins with actions that follow loss of integrity. Each arises out of the disconnection of awareness from the essence of being, results in feeling discontent, and is your usual driving force toward finding a way to feel whole again.

Feeling whole, cared for and fulfilled, you also feel sexy. That's the starting point for solutions to every problem. Heartlessness and disconnection (loss of integrity) create problems, all of which get better when you bring heart to bear on them. Heart, with or without money, improves every problem that heartlessness created. Problems express the darkness of discontent. **Love brings light to darkness. Love cures ills. Only love casts no shadow**.

Many people think that they need to become 'better' persons, but they don't. Lucky for you, better has always been within you and within every person. You need to rediscover it. It's been waiting for your attention all your life, just a tiny bit deeper inside than you're used to taking your awareness.

The world that works for all has always been a possibility, because that world already exists within your core, and is therefore translatable into a vision in your mind, from which it becomes the words you speak and the hands you use to confirm it in action. In every age in history, some people chose to live that kind of life. It's an individual choice each one of them made then, and that each one of you can make now, while you live.

Most of the work toward it is homework you do on yourself. Its discovery, through inner experience, reveals to you even more of your magnificent total being. You then see and know it in others automatically. It takes one to know one. Magnificence is within all, and magnificence beholds that. Your state of being creates your world.

You can only give what you have. If you want to give money, first get it. That's true for whatever you want to give the world. To give peace, care, light or magnificence to the world, first know, own and be peace, care, light and magnificence in the world of your own being. Embody it. Then share it. If no one has peace, where's the peace in the world supposed to come from? If you want to give love, first get, feel and be it in your life. If you want to give light, kindness and compassion, first get and feel them in your self. Sharing them is second nature and automatic once you embody them.

Discover more of what you have and are, so that you are and have more to give. I told you about the vision that I live into. In my vision, 8 billion people live

- Their lives lit up from within
- Harmoniously together, globally
- With all of everyone's basic needs met
- Sustainably on this delicate, natural planet

8 billion people are on the team to get it done. Each of us can do more homework to live more brightly lit up from within. That's how we make it happen. We don't need outside help. We need inside help. The only useful outside help is someone who can remind us and maybe show us how to focus our attention inwardly where the help we need is waiting. How are you doing as a member of the team of 8 billion who live lit up from within? Each of us will always be a student of the light of life that is our common inner master.

Never Wrong

In spite of what parents, siblings, playmates, teachers and other people have told you, and in spite of what you believe and tell yourself, there's never ever been anything wrong with you. There's never been anything wrong with any human being. However, you have lost touch with life, felt bad, had nasty thoughts, said hurtful words and did destructive acts with destructive results. Maybe you also failed to take responsibility, and blamed the consequences of your acts on others. Given all that, how can I say that there's never been anything wrong with you? Good question. Here's my answer.

You're not your feelings, your thoughts, your words, your actions or their consequences. On your deepest and most powerful level, your essential self, you're awareness and life energy, always beyond what you feel, think, say and do. When you connect to your essential self, you find that it remains unaffected by anything you felt, thought, said or did, and by anything others said or did to you. You're formless energy and pure awareness.

When you reconnect awareness with itself and with the energy of life, you discover by your experience that your essence has never been affected by anything you've ever done, anything anyone has ever done to you, and anything that's ever happened to you. Your essence remains unchanged and unchangeable because that is its nature.

Connected, you'll also get that your disconnection from your self drove your negative feelings, mean thoughts, unkind words and hurtful deeds. Here's the kicker. As you reconnect more and more deeply to your essential self, you increasingly find that how you feel, what you think, what you say and what you do change powerfully in a positive direction. Insight cures ignorance. Light is the cure for darkness. As you feel completely whole and cared for in your essential self, you recognize more and more deeply that it's always been this way. You just hadn't noticed it so clearly before. Now that you know from your experience that you ARE always perfectly cared for, you no longer need to desperately seek ways to GET taken care of.

Fulfilled and cared for, you can now extend to others the care you receive from life and feel in your being, independent of your circumstances. It's the personal transformation of the world. **Transformation is sexy**.

It begins with the transformation of YOUR inner world, which then expands into your outside world. Insight transforms you. Insight alone consistently does so. Truth is, it's not REALLY transformation. You don't turn into something or someone you were not. It IS a deeper discovery of your wholeness, your being and your full, eternal presence, which appears to others on the outside as a transformation.

This is not my pipe dream. What I say comes from personal experience. Remember that I came from war, from poverty, from hunger, from abandonment and from rejection. I was not born into a peaceful world, or into wealth, influence, status, care, acceptance, inclusion or belonging.

With a war-torn, chaotic, humble beginning, a six year-old child's hope that there must be a way to live in harmony and the determination that I'd find out how SHOULD have been a pipe dream, and I a mess. But I have the best life imaginable, beyond my wildest dreams. I've spent my life single-mindedly pursuing every avenue available to me for finding the answer to that early hope of harmony.

Even the dramas and traumas of my early life became gifts to me. They drove me to search and find something better. It's been a journey from hell to heaven, war to peace, darkness to light, emptiness to fulfillment, poverty to prosperity, fear to courage, and hate to love. I know that road.

No matter how dark your life seems to be, the light you seek is closer than you think. It's right under your nose and closer to you than your breath. If you want that, I'll go with you into your deepest darkness and together we'll walk back into the light you are. What's in me is also in you. What all the great masters spoke of is in your nature. It was available to those living there and then. It is also available to every one of 8 billion people living here and now. That's because master and mastery are already present (perhaps asleep) within each one of you, each one of us.

To find it, you have to find your starting point. Do you want to know the starting point for this journey to your deepest self? Focus on the ache you feel in your heart when you feel blue, lonely, sad, sorry, empty, yearning, longing or hurt. What is your word for the feeling that us your access to the journey into the light you are?

There's never been anything wrong with anyone, ever, no matter what anyone ever told you, you told yourself, someone said about someone else, and no matter what you ever read or heard from anyone anywhere.

Let me make one more point. Most of you, about 95% according to some experts, will do more to escape from pain than you will do to catch joy. You live your life from crisis to crisis. It's a life of emergencies that ends in death, without a vision of possibility for life. Become one of the 5% that chases and catches life.

One evening many years ago, I had the good fortune to listen to Linus Pauling, who, with an IQ of 200, was one of the smartest persons of the 20th century. The only winner of two unshared Nobel Prizes (Chemistry and Peace), I greatly admired this man. During his talk, Pauling said, "My reason for the work I do is to minimize the suffering in the world." I'd heard other people make similar statements, but when Pauling said it, it hit me like a ton of bricks that his noble goal was not effectively focused. Here's why.

Maximizing joy more effectively minimizes suffering than minimizing suffering ever could. When you maximize joy, suffering automatically ends, because maximizing joy is the light that dispels the darkness of suffering. When you enjoy, you don't suffer. You cannot feel inspired to be alive and be depressed about being alive at the same time. Chasing love works better than fighting hate. Bringing light is more effective than trying to remove darkness, which is nothing to begin with. Both within us and around us in the world, it will always work better to feed the good wolf than to punish the bad wolf.

11

ILLNESS:
Breakdown

HEALTHY AND SEXY SHOW UP as energetic, vital, present, light, easy, clear, whole, radiant, integrated, charged, enthusiastic, inspired, jazzed and natural. You can describe health as the state of alignment with each of the eight parts of nature and human nature. When you live in line with the following 8 parts, you get total sexy health:

1. Aware of inner peace and wholeness

2. Lit up with light, radiant and energized

3. Inspired and in creative mental mode

4. Your body fed and fit for action balanced with rest

5. Survival mind directed toward safety in which you can thrive

6. Integrated into social groups globally responsible to both self and nature

7. Living sustainably in your natural environment

8. At peace with the BIG picture

As health goes down, sexy goes down. Illness shows up most obviously as low energy, confused, anxious, irritable or violent. Illness is departure from the natural functioning of one or more parts of nature and human nature. Departure from each one of the eight parts of total sexy health produces a different kind of illness.

Internal and infinite awareness

Both of these are one and beyond opposites. Awareness is beyond life and death, time and space, and all other polar contrasts, including health and illness. Awareness never gets sick. Undifferentiated and without inside dimensions or outside surfaces, awareness cannot be damaged or broken down in any way.

For something to break down, it must have form. Breakdown is loss, change or damage of form. What's formless to begin with can't lose its form. However, a pain with many names including 'emptiness', heartache and 'dark night of the soul' results when your awareness drifts away from the core of your being and you disconnect from or lose touch with the feeling in your core. Disconnected, you feel this pain, which can also be described as a feeling of general discontent.

Most people remember feeling this pain in their chest when they lose something or someone dear to them. Although you feel it in your chest, this pain is not about heart, lung, digestive or other physical problem.

Before addressing this chest pain, check out the physical aspect with your health care professional, to be sure that what you feel is NOT a physical issue that requires a physical intervention. Once you know it's not a physical problem, determine if you can address it as an issue of discontent.

Physical disease and discontent or emptiness have completely different origins and respond to completely different interventions. Discontent is the painful symptom of separation of your awareness from the core of your being. You're fortunate that it's painful because without pain to get your attention, you'd never be alerted to deal with your disconnection. You'd never find your way back to the core of your being and the rich feelings of peace and wholeness that live there.

Additional names for the discontent that follows inner disconnection from self include heartbreak, emptiness, blues, yearning, loneliness, sorrow, separate and more. I'll post other names on the website: www.totalsexyhealth.com. You can add other names to the list. Send them to me, and I'll post them for all to share.

On that site is also an introduction to the most important not-had conversation, which 8 billion people deserve to have. It goes to the core of every single problem humans have ever created as individuals or groups. I've had this conversation with several thousand people, and every one of them was able to identify the feeling of heartache. None know its purpose; they don't usually like the feeling; and they do whatever it takes to remain distracted from it. Or they blame it on some person or event. They're shocked to know that other than being alive, this is the greatest gift they've been given. They get a lot out of the conversation, and many have told me that in the less than 2 hours it takes to have it, their life changed forever in the best possible way.

In my view, discontent is the great enigma of human existence. Here's a way to put it in context. You know what to do when you're hungry, thirsty, tired or in danger. When it's too hot or too cold, you know what to do. When you need air or your bladder is full, you know what to do.

When your heart aches, you don't know what it is and don't have a clue what to do with it. No culture in the world teaches how to quench the thirst of the heart. Savvy manipulators take advantage of your confusion about the nature of this ache. They use your ache to coerce, exploit and enslave you in a thousand different ways.

I work to make the conversation about the thirst of the heart: its nature, its function and its relief the most popular topic on the planet, because it holds the answers to most of your important unsolved problems. You'll be able to effectively do what needs to be done in the world only after you've answered the central question of your being and existence. That answer is not in words. It is a matter of experiential knowing.

Deep down, you know that you don't need more stuff or more activities. You need a deeper appreciation of what you already have: the wealth and wonder of life in human form. From a place of appreciation, most of your big and small problems become easy to fix. Let me know through the website when you want to have that conversation.

Disconnection of your awareness from the infinite BIG PICTURE leads to discontent, instability and mistrust and sets the stage for anxiety, fear and all the other negative emotions that interfere with living the life you want and deserve.

Life

Life is light, and light makes you feel light. The sunlight energy of life is so light, in fact, that it can lift your heavy body all the way up to the top of your head. It is lighter than helium. The energy of life weighs nothing but runs everything in your body, using the genetic program it created and perfected for that purpose over several billion years.

Life energy is formless and indestructible. Like awareness, but less subtle, it cannot break down, get sick or die. It is beyond circumstance, trauma and drama. The shape of your body state of your mind, nature of your social groups and quality of your natural environment do not affect the energy that is your life.

In other words, your body could be completely wrecked and on its way out, your mind and thoughts could be entirely disorganized and your social and natural surroundings could be a mess, but your life energy would not be affected in the least by any of these. That's why I call life 'perfect health.' Nothing can hurt or harm life energy.

Life, the perfect standard of health, is always inside of every bit of your body. It makes healing from physical, mental, social and environmental illnesses possible. If life were not the standard of perfect health within you, it would be almost impossible to recover your health once you had lost it.

When you focus awareness on your body and lose awareness of the energy of life, you feel heavy because the body is heavy. Awareness of life lightens and enlightens you. Thoughts are light and heavy, too. Depressed, dark, negative, thoughts make you feel heavy. Light, positive, inspired thoughts make you feel light.

When you feel tired and you tell yourself how tired you feel, you feel even more tired. When you stay with breath or the feeling of life, your body can be tired and you can still feel light and be alert and fresh, and find that you have far more energy than you think.

Recently, I was part of a team challenge in which we carried heavy loads, first up a mountain and then back down again (yeah, go figure!). We noticed that focusing on how tired our body felt slowed us down further. However, focusing on breathing lightly and feeling life enabled us to turn the trudge up the mountain into a dance, freed more energy, and made the task easier. A team member proposed that four of us get in a circle and take three deep breaths together, to shift our focus from body to air. It took about 20 seconds. We all felt remarkably refreshed. You're capable of much more than you think. Your stamina and performance depend to a large degree on where you focus.

In the past, I traveled internationally six to nine months every year about 15 years in a row, often did four presentations plus media every day, got up at 4 am and sometimes returned bone-weary, brain-fried at 1 am after talks and dialog with my audiences.

One day, it occurred to me that life never sleeps and never gets tired. Then I discovered that when I focus my awareness on life or breathing lightly, I remain alert and focused even when physically dead tired. This enabled me to stay inspired and inspiring and helped me sustain a nearly impossible travel schedule without burning out.

People often ask me how I have so much energy at my age. My answer is that I'm clear and free of doubt about who I am and what I'm here for. I stay in touch with life, my source of power, instead of dissipating energy complaining how tough my amazingly beautiful and lit up life is.

Once you learn, practice and get good at focusing awareness on the sunshine energy that is your life, you'll be surprised how much more staying power you have than you ever believed. **Life is the energy that lights, enlightens, uplifts, inspires, powers and empowers you, and makes you sexy.**

Mind 1 and 2

Mind 1 is creativity. Creativity bridges life and the world. It's inspired, optimistic and filled with surprise and wonder. When stress threatens your survival, it takes over your attention, and you lose your focus on your creativity.

When this happens, you may fail to see options and lose your sense of meaning and purpose. Then you're more likely to get depressed. Feeling stressed and depressed may eventually lead to self-destructive behavior.

Make sure that you have creative projects to focus on before and when there's stress in your life. Creative pursuits diminish the power that stress, conflict, doubts and dilemmas can have over you.

Negative feelings lead to negative thoughts, negative words and negative actions that foster negative consequences. Disconnect from internal awareness, life and creativity, and you set the stage for destructive processes, which expressed, create problems in the world, including war, injustice and environmental destruction.

Mind 2 is for survival. There are bugs in paradise. Changes and surprises trigger fight, flight, freeze or withdrawal reactions within you and result in high levels of stress. Short term, stress prepares your body for intense physical survival activity.

Long-term threats to survival, even when only imagined, wear you down, overwhelm you and burn you out. Exhausted, tiny additional stresses can make your body sick, collapse its ability to function and rapidly destroy your body.

When necessary, take decisive protective actions with confidence. When possible, use creativity and foresight to preemptively create protected safe surroundings that minimize stress, threats and dangers. In safe environments, stresses are occasional. Between crises, you have time to rest, heal, sleep, play and relax. Then, situations that you saw as stresses that you must face, fight and overcome in order to survive can become challenges and adventures that you gladly take on with excitement for growth.

Some experts call 'stress' those situations you didn't choose and see as negative. They call situations you choose and welcome in order to challenge yourself for growth and fun '*eustress*'. Looked at this way, stress victimizes you, and *eustress* builds you and makes you more resilient.

Body

Where in the body does illness begin? What exactly is the nature of physical disease? If we're to find cures for incurable diseases, these are important questions. The answer is as surprising as it is simple. Sunlight energy constructs your body out of oxygen, water, food nutrients and other molecules made by plants, herbs, spices and/or animals. Life uses your genetic program to create and repair your cells, tissue, glands, organs and systems. Most of you are born relatively healthy and get sick only later on.

What happens when you get sick? At what level of body organization does disease begin? The formless awareness that is your foundation can never get sick because its nature is unchangeable. Life also never gets sick because it is formless energy that powers all your internal chemistry but is unaffected by the activity that it catalyzes in your body. Sub-atomic particles never get sick. Electrons never get heart attacks, cancer, arthritis or diabetes. Neither do protons, neutrons or atoms. Even molecules never get sick in any way. They just are what they are and act according to their nature.

Given these facts, you can conclude that even when you're really sick, not much in you is sick, and far more in you is healthy than is sick. Putting sickness in this perspective can give you hope. Cells, tissues, glands, organs, systems and bodies, on the other hand, do get sick. When you examine the origin of physical illness closely, you find that all physical ailments begin at the level of interactions between molecules. Illness begins with unnatural molecular interactions.

Interactions between molecules in your body occur the way they do as a result of their nature, structure, shape and properties. Natural interactions between natural molecules (molecules that exist in nature) occur in ways that allow the body to be made and function naturally, normally. We call that natural, normal state 'physical health'.

Unnatural molecules interact with body molecules in ways that are not natural, normal or healthy. They interfere with, block or derail the natural molecular interactions. And that's where the symptoms of disease begin.

First, they happen on the level of interactions between molecules.

Then they show up as abnormal cell function.

Then, tissues are affected.

Then, glands, organs or systems show signs and symptoms of abnormal interactions between molecules.

Finally, your body fails to function normally, and disease management professionals diagnose signs and symptoms and give this failure of normal functions a name: cancer, heart disease, diabetes, arthritis, dementia and so on.

After the diagnosis, they likely give you a drug that masks symptoms without fixing the root of the problem caused by unnatural (abnormal) interactions between molecules. Or, they cut out bad bits. Or, they bombard affected parts with powerfully destructive rays. To address the problem in a way that cures it at its origin, you must see to it that only natural molecules that interact naturally with each other land in your body. We call it 'living in line with nature'. Why is that important?

Life made your genetic program in nature, to construct and repair your body using only molecules that come from the natural environment. That program can't work properly when you put industrial, synthetic, unnatural molecules that never existed in nature into your body, or when you bombard your body with potent radioactive or electromagnetic rays that change molecules. Living in line with nature is your best shot at having a body that works normally. Living out of line with nature guarantees that you'll deconstruct (break down) your health. Five main ways you get ill from living out of line with nature include:

1. **Deficiency**: Inadequate intake of essential nutrient building blocks from nature, which life uses to make and repair your body. Rarely, you can also get sick from getting too much of a few of them.

2. **Toxicity**: Poisonous elements, and poisonous molecules made by microbes, plants, animals and humans. In the modern world, most illnesses result from human-made industrially produced, toxic synthetic molecules and processed, fried and damaged foods that prevent normal interactions between natural molecules in your body from taking

place. These molecules should never be put into your body in the first place.

3. **Poor digestion**: Lack of digestive enzymes, fiber and probiotics lead to both deficiency and toxicity.

4. **Impaired circulation**: Deprives cells of food and energy and allow toxic molecules and wastes to remain in tissues, where they interfere with normal interactions between molecules and compromise tissue functions.

5. **Destructive energy**: Ultraviolet, X-rays and gamma rays and radioactivity from unstable elements break bonds and create free radical reactions and unnatural molecules in your body.

When you make the effort necessary to live with your body in line with nature, you find that the problems resulting from not doing so resolve, except for the inevitable aging to which all bodies are heir. As life repairs and detoxifies your body, the physical pains you feel slowly diminish. You get your energy and normal functions back.

Group

We're better together than we are alone. We're especially good together when we live in mutual acceptance of the uniqueness of each member in the group and pool our talents for the good of all at the expense of none. We're even better and sexier together when we include every living person, globally, in our mutual acceptance and celebration of the uniqueness of each member.

You're better alone than together when the group does not accept you the way you are because of biases against what you cannot change. If you cannot belong to a group for any reason, you still belong to life, and life accepts and cares for you exactly as you are. You're also better alone than in the group if the group threatens you with expulsion and pressures you to conform in word and deed to group norms that involve disrespect and violence against life, body, nature, other groups or non-members of the group. Threats and pressure to conform can make you sick. Anxiety, fear, anger, embarrassment and shame threaten not only your health, but also disrupt the harmony and health both of other members and the group.

Relationships that lack mutual acceptance and care, and are instead based on hating and hurting, can make you sick. "You make me sick!" is a strong emotional outburst you've heard or may even have used. Sick-making social issues are especially intense when you depend on the group to survive, feel forced to be what you're not, accept what is not caring of life, and behave in ways that deny and destroy life.

Young children are vulnerable and easy to indoctrinate. As an adult, reexamine what you were forced to comply with as a child. Keep helpful knowledge, and discard the rest. **It's sexy to re-examine and re-write your life as an adult**.

My early childhood was filled with anxiety, fear, anger, mistrust and pain. I knew the terror of war, lack of food, bullying, abandonment and rejection. Years later, based on insights from inner experiences and a different outside world, I re-wrote my story. I looked at old beliefs I held, compared them to the world in which I now live, dumped those that no longer apply, and created new ones more in line with the present in which I live. Along the way, I met several excellent mentors who helped me far more than they'll ever know. More than 9,000 pages of written material are partial proof of my rewritten life. I was born in an ugly war and now I live in delicious peace. It's been a profound, rich journey that gets better and better with time.

Find your group or live alone. Either way, be yourself. Don't compromise being who you are and what you know is true. Question what you're told. Don't be fooled by sweet talk. The reformer Martin Luther suggested that, "When you're with people, don't watch their mouth. Watch their fists (actions)." Actions speak louder than words.

What people DO expresses far more clearly what they stand for than all the fancy words they use. Words can whitewash and deceive you. So can 'principles'. One great social illness is the 'loyalty principle', expressed as 'My country, my race, my religion, right or wrong!' When you're loyal to what's true, you build positive and life-affirming groups and nations. When you're loyal to a group and turn a blind eye to actions out of line with truth, you erode the integrity of the members, the group and the environments they act in. That kind of loyalty enslaves. Marketing deception, political conflicts and wars rob you of choice about health and quality of life.

Know and act on truth. It sets you free. **Personal and social integrity are both sexy and healthy**.

Nature

Nature is both your father and mother and provides all resources that fulfill your physical and energetic needs. Nature is huge and we humans are tiny in it. All humans make up only 0.1%, fungus & bacteria about 35%, and plants about 40% of the total biomass of Earth. We're not so big!!!

Overuse, careless use, waste and recreational destruction of resources lead toward a planet you can no longer live on. The fishing industry decimated fish so rapidly that researchers predict that within three decades, no fish will live in the oceans.

Industry pollutes air, water and soils more and more rapidly, with acidic carbon dioxide and removal of alkaline oxygen. This decimates coral reefs, extincts species, changes climate, increases weather extremes, decreases oxygen and increases physical degeneration. The climate changes toward more widespread insect-borne illnesses, environmental collapses on land and in oceans, and more severe weather patterns.

At present, more and more value is being placed on banks and money and less and less on human, animal and plant life. Governments concern themselves mostly with economic indicators that measure how the banks are doing, but have nothing in place to measure how each citizen is doing, especially in terms of internal quality of life. They also lack indicators of how nature is doing. They protect money and banks, but neglect the living creatures. People are stressed and on edge. More and more people flip out. Concerns over terror and violence become more and more ominous, and even young adults who grew up in affluent situations are more and more discontent.

When you define nature as an enemy to be predicted, controlled, tamed, conquered and exploited, industrial pollution and environmental destruction follow. The damage that food processing and preparation do to foods damages health, as do toxic energies, atoms, elements, molecules, microbes, plants and animals. Sickness results from insufficient oxygen and too much carbon dioxide. Water shortages and floods, crop failures, soil erosion and depletion, hunger, dehydration, starvation and pesticide-poisoned foods cause great suffering and illness.

Environmental illness also includes mental forms. Some of them stem from the burden of knowing that you live unsustainably. Some come from knowing how you deceive the people you live with. Others come from knowing the results of what you do to creatures and natural environments. Freedom to cause destruction and then walk away from it without responsibility to clean up the mess you make has been the insane model of the past few centuries.

Even though this is not sustainable, oligarchs fight ferociously to continue life-destroying ways of thinking and acting. The *inconvenient truth*: Everything works long-term only if and when citizens and rulers care for all humans and all of life on this excellent, elegant, fragile, delicate, graceful, drop-dead gorgeously sexy planet.

The leadership model of one person telling many other people what to think, say and do is a model that makes sense only in emergencies and crises, and only short-term. Even in such situations, leaders need to be qualified with long track records of caring for all the creatures they command, beginning with themselves. The ego-based leadership model has historically cast many shadows both over people and nature.

That kind of outdated, ego-based human leadership model was never the best way to enhance quality of life of family, country or planet. It runs counter to the human drive for self-determination. No leader, no matter how wise or powerful, can keep up with and direct everything by imposition from outside. It's not even possible to totally keep track of your own family. Replace this flawed, outdated leadership model with education that inspires and empowers citizens to take on personal and global self-responsibility.

What is a better model? It's what great masters and sages over the ages modeled, but we have largely overlooked. These were human beings who mastered full presence in all of their being, and taught others who wanted a life like that to do the same: to master what the masters mastered. Self-knowledge, self-mastery and self-responsibility are the keys that make this work and no quality of life is better than that. Imagine 8 billion people living fulfilled, with awareness of life directing each individual's activities. Self-mastery makes most outside control unnecessary.

When you live in awareness of life, of creative mind, of the body and its needs, and of protective mind, you become master of your world of feelings, thoughts, words, acts and consequences. When you live lit up from within, social harmony and the fulfillment of people's basic needs become a relatively easy and practical possibility. Inherent in your nature, you only have to discover that option, be present to it, and let it direct your life.

When you fail to align with nature, your emotions show up negative, unpredictable and destructive to yourself, others and the planet. When you align your life with nature, you show up calmly present, and you live life in a magnificent and masterful way.

12

DEATH:
Physical Disintegration

Perspective

WITH BIRTH COMES DEATH. You know that death is inevitable. Even though your body is temporary, you spend most of your time looking after the needs of this time-limited part of your nature. You eat, drink, breathe, sleep, dress, wash, change socks, undress and go to the toilet to take care of the needs of your body.

Looking after the body is a necessary but losing proposition, because in the end your body fails. You know it, but every time someone dies you're still surprised, and then sad, angry or mournful.

By putting everything in perspective, death teaches you how to live. The fact that some day life and your body will part company, and that the body will then break down into the elements and simple molecules from which life constructed it puts you on notice. It reminds you to examine what in your world is important and what is trivial. Without death looming, you'd waste a lot of time. You might remain forever stupid, and never examine, come to terms with or edify your stupidity. Death lets you know that your time on Earth matters. It asks you, "Who are you? What's worth doing? What is true to life? How can you best spend your time here? What is a life worth living like?"

Many people think of India as the birthplace of the exploration, by self-observation, of the inner nature of being human. The Upanishads, a rich collection of 'wisdom texts' and stories from India, came out of the inner explorations of individuals who sought to connect with the infinite within the human. Predictably, death is one of the topics.

In one of these texts, known as the Katha Upanishad, a father sends his young son, Nachiketa, to death at the angry conclusion of a disagreement between them. The boy goes to the realm of death. There he meets Yama, the King of Death, who turns out to be fully alive and also the ultimate wisdom teacher. Long story short, Nachiketa has a key question he wants answered, "When someone dies, there arises a doubt. 'He still exists,' say some. 'He does not,' say others. I want you to teach me the truth." In other words, is there existence after death? Death replies, "This doubt haunted even the old gods; the secret of death is hard to know."

He tries to distract Nachiketa with worldly pleasures, but the boy persists. "Dispel this doubt of mine, oh King of Death. Does a person live after death or does he not?" Death answers him:

"The joy of spirit ever abides, but not what seems pleasant to the senses. The wise recognize this, but not the ignorant. Wisdom and joy of spirit come through self-knowledge. Your senses take you outward, away from your wholeness and put you under my (death's) sway. The wise ones realize the timeless 'Self' hidden in the cave of the heart beyond the senses, and put death to death. When the body dies, the Self does not die because it was never born. This can't be known by thinking, but only by experience through a practice of self-knowledge guided by teachers lit up from within by life's light of Love."

This is Death's summary of the illusory nature of death.

In China and among aboriginal people, the 'ancestors' are said to be always present. In the sense of the Katha Upanishad, they are beyond the senses, beyond good and evil and beyond life and death but are present as formless awareness. What is aware and present will always be aware and present.

Awareness (or pure consciousness) can't just turn into nothing after death if it was real during life before death. Life that is energy, light, sound and feeling can't just disappear without a trace when it disconnects from the body. Energy remains energy. The atoms that make up the body don't disappear. Nature simply mixes them with the rest of the atoms on earth, and re-uses them to build other forms.

Many native tribes invite their ancestors to be present as an affirmation of this timeless truth. At their most conscious, they live their lives aware of the ancestral presence and the infinite context within which they play out their physical existence. Their reference to the ancestors' presence in their meetings gives deeper meaning and broader perspective to important considerations and impactful decisions. Some thoughtful leaders suggest that the only reason any of the ancestors ever lived is so that you could be here now. And they admonish us to show up powerful for life and grateful for the blessing of existence.

In the modern world, we observe that at the point of death, the true nature of the body shows up. It was always a physical vehicle, a complex molecular structure that life created from matter to use for physical activity, made from physical materials on a physical planet. Life grows, maintains and animates that structure for a time. When life and body separate, it becomes clear that the body was alive (with life) but was never life. It breaks back down into the elements from which it was constructed. Life becomes invisible. In truth, life, like the wind, is always invisible. We can't see it, but know its presence by the fluttering leaves on trees, waves on ocean water and clouds moving across the sky, as well as by the sound it creates as it passes through the trees in a forest. We know life's presence mainly from the animation that it catalyzes.

Essence

Something deep and essential in you was never born. Never born, that essence never dies. What exactly that is, only deep practice and the personal experience of inner self-knowledge enable you to know. It's not speculative. It does not exist in theory. It exists only in reality. When you experience it, you know it's real. When you don't experience it, you can only guess, speculate or deny. Only your deepest essence fits that description.

This doesn't mean that people have not spoken about it, or imagined it in their minds, or parroted back something that someone spoke in words FROM their experience. But the words are NOT the experience, and the words people use to express the experience of their essence are not usually the way to get you TO that essence. You know, when you experience it for yourself, that its reality is beyond sensory impressions and language.

Your desire to know it will take you toward it. By all means, make effort to get to it. If that doesn't work, ask for help. I did both. I started alone, but found that it helped greatly to work with others farther along the journey of self-knowledge than I. You choose. But don't just guess, and don't play games with yourself. Find out for real. Go deeply into your nature, and you find that life and death both come out of the same root.

From life's perspective, death is illusory. It's a surface symptom of physical appearance. From the outside, death can be dramatic and frightening, because it is final, permanent, strange and messy. You see the body of someone who 'died,' and notice that there's nobody home. A person with whom you interacted in one or more possible ways no longer responds to you in any way.

Talk, and no one answers. Push, and there's no pushback. You get no response at all. Even though the body is there, the person you knew is gone. It shocks you, even when it was expected. You can no longer connect, interact, influence or enjoy that person.

Three stories describe death. One is the outside story of the physical symptoms and signs of death as observed and interpreted through your senses. Doctors, nurses, those who looked after dying family members and people who witnessed or responded to car accidents, house fires, murder, industrial accidents, acts of terror and war described it. Several books written by medical doctors detail the sequence of processes of physical deterioration as 'death' takes place.

The second story about death is conceptual. This is a mixture of fear- or hope-based speculations, fantasies, cultural stories, religious beliefs and outright fabrications used largely to allay people's fears or perhaps to control their behavior.

The third story is the inside story of death. This is a story of awareness, as experienced by a person in the process of dying. A few books contain people's personal reports of 'near-death' experiences of dying and then returning to the world. There's also a way in which you can experience dying without dying. That's the most interesting part because it is the most practical and instructive. You can know it now.

Growing up on a farm with animals, I often observed the *external* process of dying. It's predictable, and frankly, not interesting. I'm more attracted to the profoundly personal and experiential nature of the *internal* mystery and miracle of death. What does a person who's dying experience? What will be my experience of dying? I won't know it for sure until that event takes place, but I'd like to know enough to die with a positive and fearless, accepting and calm attitude. Is that possible? Read on.

Three Stories

Outside (sensory) story: With air, water and food as building blocks, life grows your body from fertilized egg (zygote) through an entire lifetime. It begins at conception as one living cell, which fed, watered and oxygenated, divides over and over into multi-trillions of cells organized and differentiated into hundreds of specialized tissue types, each of which life constructs and regulates by turning specific genes on, off, up or down.

As you grow, mature and act in the physical world, you learn one skill and competence after another. Then, as you age and become weaker, you gradually lose some of these skills and competencies. Eventually, your body deteriorates, then fails and dies. Death ends all our skills.

This is the human life cycle. 100 billion people have lived on Earth. 8 billion live now. 92 billion have lived and died. No human living now is 500, 1,000 or 50,000 years old. Although we keep trying, no one's beat the system. Why do we keep trying? We fear death and want to conquer it. It's delusional. Dying is not a big deal. 92 billion people have died successfully. Living is the big deal.

Mental (conceptual) story: Finding meaning in life occupies a lot of human time after childhood. Dogs and trees don't bother themselves with this topic. It's a uniquely human preoccupation. Sages tell us the meaning of life exists in just being. It's less the result of thoughts or activities than of experience. Meaning is your internal foundation rather than an external edifice. It requires your presence in and awareness of your total nature. In your hectic lives of external pursuits and obsessions, you neglect the inside track of knowing and feeling present in total sexy health.

True meaning is a direct experience of being. The meaning of life is inherent in the feeling of life. Most people try to give meaning to their doing, but it's fleeting. Again and again, you find that the meaning you'd hoped to get from your doing doesn't materialize or quickly evaporates, independent even of whether you succeed or fail. Either way, you feel let down. Then you harness this letdown for your next futile doing-based project.

When you lose awareness of the experience of your sexy being, you lose your inherent feeling of meaning, and can become desperate or hopeless. You might try to explain it away, distract yourself from it, deny, or ignore or find someone or something to blame it on. Or you might grab on to a set of beliefs. The fact is that no thought-based way exists for true relief from the feelings of loss, pain, grief and emptiness that your disconnection from your life creates within you.

Some people who feel hopeless because they've lost their self-connection and see no future to look forward to or live into, destroy their body by suicide, or destroy others by acts of crime, violence and terror. What a waste of magnificence!! Out of touch with life, a mind poisoned by discontent can abuse or destroy bodies before they wear out.

Life makes the ideas of suicide, violence and terror possible, but life does not come up with those ideas. Mind disconnected from life does. Life always unconditionally loves and takes care of your body, no matter what you feel, think, say or do. Even when you get the idea that you hate your life, it loves and cares for you. **Feeling life, the source of meaning, is sexy**.

Inside (experiential) story: The inside story of dying follows awareness as it moves back to its source. If you think of yourself as 'practical', you might consider the topic as a waste of time. Or you might be uncomfortable with it. For many years, I thought so too, as did my siblings and parents. But it turns out that in truth, it's more real and practical than what you consider practical.

All knowledge results from becoming aware of, observing, and learning about whatever you focus on. Expertise and special skills result from repeatedly focusing awareness. The inside story of dying is one such area of focus.

Most of your life, you live with your awareness focused on what surrounds you, who surrounds you, and what you think and feel about what and who surrounds you. Dying involves a process in which your focus of awareness shifts from all of these back to its deepest primary source. The process of dying proceeds through a sequence of steps. During that process, your awareness detaches itself, in the following general order, from

- The surfaces of things in the world in which you live: images, colors, movements, sounds, tones, smells, tastes and touch; then from
- Your thoughts, concepts, ideas, beliefs, memories and imaginings; then from
- The sensations of your body; then from
- The light, sound and feeling of life energy; and into
- Internal awareness, then expanding outward into infinite awareness

Struggle: Some people struggle in the dying process. You can see it in hospice work. They fight like crazy to hold on and do not want to let go. Of course, they can't hold on and sooner or later they do have to let go. Why do some people struggle to hold on, while others let go without resistance and pass on peaceful and comfortable? The answer is simple. It's difficult and we struggle when we have to let go of what we're attached to by positive or negative emotions. If you fear death at the time of death, you'll resist it. Wanting to stay in the world while leaving it is a fight you can't win and are guaranteed to lose. A death struggle results from your attachment to the world of surfaces and things; your thoughts, concepts, beliefs, memories and imaginings; your body; and the energy of life.

What are you attached to? What don't you want to let go of and leave? What do you hold yourself responsible for? What unfinished business do you have? What have you left undone? What amends do you need to make? What rules and habits are you locked into? Death will break your will, defy your rules and erase your beliefs. It sounds harsh, but it's not. It's easier and more beautiful than you would ever think or imagine.

Know

How can you know death before death? As writer of this book, how do I know? After all, I haven't died. Am I just imagining this? Am I fearful of dying and need to make sense of what makes no sense? Do I need a straw to grasp in the hope that it'll protect me from the inevitable demise looming in my future? These are good questions. How do I know? I know from my own experience. I know because I wanted to know. I know because I asked and searched. I didn't want someone to feed me answers that I'd have to accept on faith without proof. I wanted direct knowledge.

Do you want to know for sure, from your experience? If you do, take time for solitude and internalize your awareness more deeply. Sit still and do nothing. Look, listen and feel inward. Become aware of your inner light, inner sound and inner feeling. Focus on that which is aware of inner light, sound and feeling. The awareness behind these energies is who you are. It is also your source and your final destination.

People find sitting still difficult. We get bored when it gets quiet inside because it seems like there's nothing going on, and we're addicted to crisis- and stimulation-based change. Fall in love with that 'nothing', because it shows that your awareness is moving in the right (internal) direction. Notice how composed and calm the nothing is, how much space is in it, and how deeply you can unwind, rest, slow down and de-stress. Relax into it. No pills needed.

Between the outer world of crises, emergencies, stresses and incessant activities and the inner world of peace, presence and feeling unconditionally cared for is a 'no man's land' where there is neither. That's what you call 'boredom'. You're actually just calming down. Only in calmness can you contact the greater being, your source. In calm space (that you find boring), you discover your magnificent essence. Sit and be with it.

Deepen self-knowledge until you become aware of your inner awareness, and then let that awareness expand endlessly outward into the infinity that embraces all things, all people, all creatures, all nature and all the solar system, galaxy and universe. Embrace all aspects of nature and human nature. Embrace what is, as it is.

The Greek philosopher Socrates had two pieces of advice. The first one flew by us all in high school in Western countries. It was, "Know thyself!" Sounded good, but no one told you what he might have meant by it, what it would entail in practice or how to proceed to 'know yourself.' He didn't say, "Know everything EXCEPT thyself!" That's how we spend our lives. What sages and masters told us to put first, we put last.

Socrates also said, "The unexamined life is not worth living." Have you heard that one? What's it mean to 'examine' your life? It's easy. You don't have to poke it. Just be with it. Be still. Be present in it. Focus on and be aware of life. Increase your depth of awareness of it. Be it. Let go and relax more deeply. Be the presence of life in human form. Be present in the presence of the life you are. Be whole, not by making up and memorizing thoughts about being whole, but by actually feeling whole within your being.

This is how you get to know yourself. This is how you come to know how rich, deep and full of peace and love and joy you are. It is also how you come to know what in you is not and cannot be touched by death. It's how you find, in the depth of your experience of life and of awareness, that death is not the end, has no dominion and truly has no sting. Death cannot, does not, and never exists in the realm of either life or awareness.

Fear of death comes from lack of knowledge of the truth of life and awareness. When you make time to practice self-knowledge and commit to the discovery of the nature of these two, you will in time and with practice find that death is your return to life. It is the return of your awareness into the energy of life and then into itself. It can separate from the body but not from itself. And 'it' is the core you. In inner light, sound and feeling, there's no darkness, silence or emptiness. In inner life, there is no end of life. In inner life, there is no death. Check it out. Maybe it's time to get to know your self more deeply. It'll transform the way in and depth to which you know your self. Then all else, as promised by great teachers, will fall into place or be 'added unto you.'

Difference

Is there a difference between self-knowledge of life, and death? Good question. There is no difference in the experience, but allow me to point out a couple of differences in their contexts.

Voluntary and involuntary: When you take up the practice of self-knowledge, it's a voluntary decision you make. You choose. You decide to make time for it or to put it off. Many folks do one and many do the other. No one can force you into the inner journey. On the outside, someone can hold a gun to your head and force you to go, stop, turn right or turn left. When someone tries to force you to bring your awareness inside, you can say "Sure thing, boss," but refuse to comply in your mind. You remain internally free to blow off the coercion.

Dragging a horse to water does not make it drink. When it becomes thirsty, it will drink. If you put salt in its food, you can speed the thirst. The salt in your food is that ache or restless empty feeling in your chest. Taking your awareness deeper inside, you will find the 'water' that quenches that 'thirst of the heart'.

You have to come up with your own reason for taking up the practice of self-knowledge. Once you know that your restless heart feeling is calling your awareness to come back to your core, you've identified why you need such a practice. That feeling of emptiness reminds and nags you whenever you lose one of your distractions. It urges you from the center of your being to bring your focus back home into awareness of your source.

Practicing self-knowledge is good for getting to know life more deeply and more fully. It is also preparation. Through it, you become more comfortable with the inevitability of your body dying, because you already know the journey. But, you choose to practice it, voluntarily, or not.

On the other hand, you don't have a choice over whether to die or not when your time comes. Without a self-knowledge practice, the process will be new to you and it will not be pleasant because all your fears and attachments will surface at a time when you no longer have choice. You can't control the dying process. If you have no familiarity with your inner nature, dying is uncharted territory, and losing control of everything you thought you were in control of is likely to intensely frighten you.

Someone told me a story of a medical doctor in the UK who collected dying people's last utterances. Do you know what the most common one was? You might laugh when I tell you. It's funny. The doctor found the most common last expression of people as they died was, "Oh shit!!" Why? All your life, you think and act as though you're in control. At the time of death, you realize as you lose it that you never had control, ever. You realize that your life, the ability to think and what you were able to do were unearned gifts that life and awareness bestowed on you. Knowing this while you live might help to make you feel even more grateful for every single thing you are, have, do and live surrounded by. Really, everything!!!

Come back and don't come back: When you practice self-knowledge, you deliberately detach and withdraw your awareness from the outside world, your mind and your body and bring it to rest in formless, indestructible life and awareness. When you're done with your practice, you bring your awareness back out into your life, body, mind, social group and world. You get to 'leave the world' and you get to come back.

This journey in and out can become a well-trod path for you. You learn to move your awareness at will to any one of these levels of your existence. You learn to function at all of these levels. You learn to be aware of these levels of existence all at the same time. Some people call this simultaneous presence the 'cherished state.' In that state, you're living fully present in all of existence.

Imagine what it might be like to be fully present in your being AND fully present in the world. In that state, you can pretty much write your ticket regarding how your life is going to go. Because it is so rich, I wish for you that kind of existence, but you will have it only if you wish that kind of existence for yourself.

On the other hand, at the point of death, the awareness you are withdraws from the outside world, your mind, body, feelings and life and drops into formless, indestructible awareness from which it does not return again to life, body, mind and world. Without knowing the nature of that journey, you're likely to be scared by your complete loss of power over what's happening.

By becoming more present to all levels of your existence, you create a lighter, richer, more fulfilling and more abundant life now and a far easier transition when your time to give up your body comes. It's not just easier for you but it's also easier for family and friends. You model living in acceptance of the whole package, and share with them the wisdom of self-knowledge. **Equanimity is massively and masterfully sexy.** You help make their lives lighter, richer, and fuller, and your death far less devastating.

No Death

Living calmly with full acceptance of your mortality in the face of all of life's challenges including aging, loss of faculties and death is sexy. You'll find it difficult to live calmly in the face of these if you don't know the source of calmness within you that is safely beyond them all.

To be present in action in the physical world while at the same time remaining aware of the big picture stillness within which that action occurs is sexy. To be aware of formless and formed, both of which you always are, is highly sexy because it's the most powerful and conscious mastery a human being can have. That which is formless within you is also beyond death. What has no form can never lose its form.

Great sages and masters throughout history have helped people come to terms with death by deepening their connection with the deathless core life energy. An example of their view on dying is the words of Lebanese poet Kahlil Gibran's '*Prophet*', who, asked about the secret of death, replies: "You would know the secret of death. But how shall you find it unless you seek it in the heart of life."

You may not have thought of them as sexy, but masters are the sexiest human beings on record because they live their lives aligned with all of nature and their nature. This is why they're so attractive, radiant and powerful.

Although there is no death at death, there IS a change in where the focus of awareness goes. Know and accept the truth of your nature. Be wise, and practice bringing your awareness home to its source while you live. Live fully present. Get used to moving awareness in and out as well as expanding it from the center outward to include everything. Get good at doing so. Master full, conscious, deliberate presence in all that you are. Dying for you will become easy or at least easier.

Those who live in the line of fire, dangers and enemies that threaten physical survival, like soldiers, firemen, police and other first responders, learn to stay fully present in life in the midst of chaos and crisis on a daily basis. Living fully present, *you* can take that fearless presence into your final transition.

When you consider all things, you find that love casts no shadows and has no adverse side effects. In love, there is no death. In life, there is no death. In creativity, there is no death. In awareness, there is no death. All these, formless and eternal, never change and are indestructible.

Thoughts, bodies, social systems and natural systems, on the other hand, have form, change, and will eventually lose their form. What you call death applies to forms but does not apply to the greater and more powerful reality that has no form: love, life, creativity and awareness. You can live with great security and peace in these, knowing that death is an external phenomenon that has no bearing on your internal core reality. What a profound contrast!! Your internal reality is indestructible. Get to know it.

13

MASTERY & MASTERS:
Full Presence

10,000 Hours

IN HIS BOOK "OUTLIERS", AUTHOR Malcolm Gladwell suggests that if you spend 10,000 hours immersed in or focused on a topic, you develop greatness. If you spend one hour every day of the week on the topic, greatness will take you just over 27 years. At 8 hours/day, 5 days/week, like a full-time job, it would take 4.8 years to develop the 10,000 hour level of greatness. It's about how long it takes to earn a Bachelor's degree.

In truth, the number of hours is less important than your immersion and your depth of focus. Both depend on the intensity of your passion for the topic. Also, there's an issue of how much learning is academic and how much is practical, hands-on, action-based, embodied and experiential.

While you can argue the exact number, it's common sense that when you've focused 10,000 hours on a topic, you'll have more than just a passing knowledge of it. You'll know the topic better than 99% of the population, and you can listen to and learn from the 1% that still knows more than you. This was a mentor's advice to me three decades ago, after I'd written my first book on health and was nervous about getting up in front of people to speak. His advice helped me to overcome my fear of public exposure.

What topic have you spent 10,000 hours exploring? For one thing, you're the master of the experiences you've had from the time of your conception until now. You're in your life, mind, body, social group and natural setting 24/7/365 every year of your time here. You may not pay attention to everything all the time or master every aspect of your life, but you know what you know. Your being is your true greatness. Your story is a story of being alive and human, with all of its challenges and all of its joys.

You may not yet have mastered full presence in all of your being, but you're the expert of your story so far. What other topics have you been learning for 10,000 hours or more? You know it better than I. Take time to make a list of what these topics are. It may help you identify the direction in which you can go to develop your quality of life as well as your livelihood. It may also bring into focus what you have talent for and can successfully contribute to the world. As you do that, you may also be able to identify the resources you need to live a full life in all its aspects.

To illustrate, let me tell you a bit about my sets of 10,000 hours. In addition to my life story, here are some of my areas of mastery. Born in the chaos of war and its aftermath, my focus from early on was on what's true and reliable. I needed to know. I felt that I couldn't count on the people and places of my early childhood. I was drawn to learn science to find out how the world and things work. Then I went to biological sciences to find out how creatures work. Then I got into psychology to find out how thinking works. Finally, I focused on self-knowledge to find out how I work, which turned out to be my most important area of study.

I've put more than 10,000 hours into human nature, nature and health. Sub-topics within these three main topics include writing, public speaking, research, education, personal development, consulting, problem solving, humor, process development and product formulation. I have basic building and gardening skills. My areas of greatest interest are education, peace and contentment, health, environment, and energy. Having been born in the darkness of war and found my way back to the light of peace, I can help you on your journey from darkness to light and war to peace.

Mastery

To live a spectacularly well-balanced life of greatness, you have to master two things.

First, work on self-mastery (greatness) to become fully present in all of your being. This takes care of your internal personal life.

Second, work on mastery of a skill or specialty that you can offer to the world. Become really good at it, so people will prefer you as a provider of that skill or specialty. This will take care of the needs of your body and your family: air, water, food, fitness, clothing, shelter, children, education, and so on.

Mastery is NOT just a matter of 10,000 hours, but is also a high level of knowledge and competence. With these comes confidence in your ability to work with all aspects of the topics you've mastered. Mastery is both academic and practical; both learning and teaching; both questions and answers. Mastery, in the final analysis, is a state of being. You occupy and embody your mastery. You own it and it owns you. Your mastery comes to expression in how you show up in the ever-changing world in which you live.

Mastery is not only a matter of time and focus, but also a matter of passion and interest. What do you bring to your inquiry? How fully do you give yourself to it? Your intent, and the quality of your teachers influence your mastery. Fake students hook up with fake masters. Mediocre students settle for mediocre masters. Eager full-on students find full-on eager masters. Both state of being and intent, as student or master, dictate to whom you're attracted and who's attracted to you.

The interest and desire that, as a student, you bring to a master is as important as the mastery that a master brings to you. Some people aren't open to learning and so are not teachable, even by a perfect master. Be open and teachable. Like every person, you have a lot to unlearn and to learn. Strive for mastery in what you do, especially in total sexy health, which gives you the strongest internal, personal foundation on which you then build a highly successful life.

Give priority to this kind of mastery, because it's central to everything you do with your time in the world. How fully you show up in the events in your life has a lot to do with how well you will do and what kind of leadership you'll provide. Don't think you know enough. There's always more. Be eager to learn more. Make mistakes, not on purpose, but in the process. You can never learn less. If you stay focused on your goals, you can fail your way to success. Keep going. Fall in love with making effort.

Openness to learning is sexy. Listen!! Every story contains in it a carrot and a stick, a vision and a threat, an inspiration and a warning. What are these in the conversations that you have? It's been said that a master can learn from everyone including a fool, but a fool cannot learn from anyone, not even himself. It's meant to be funny, but there's truth in it.

In my way of thinking, a master is greater than an expert and an expert is different from a mentor. In the time in which we live, however, we use these designations more or less interchangeably. It's my impression that in street understanding, masters embody and live their field, topic or message, while experts tend to specialize in theory, with or without hands-on experience. A <u>mentor</u> is more practical, coaching you to do what he/she has already done.

Your limitation is that you can take others only as far as you've gone. You can teach only what you know. The adage that you cannot give what you do not have applies to money but also to knowledge, expertise and mastery. Only a master can teach mastery. Only a master models and encourages students to master mastery.

Experts' teachings are limited to the limits of their expertise, and some experts won't teach all they know because they don't want to create their own competition (scarcity thinking). Some 'experts' will not allow their students to shine. Only they get to shine in their tribe. It is common for experts to have agendas that take away from their ability to give you what's best for you when it's not best for them. Watch for and be alert to such conflicts of interest.

Aim for mastery in your life. Master what the masters mastered. Embody total sexy health by being and living fully present in all of your human nature and bringing your full presence of being into your doing in your social and natural settings.

Master

A master has mastered something. He/she knows the topic inside out and embodies it. In total sexy health—our topic here—mastery is an embodiment. You are it, live it, own it, breathe it and do it. You can't settle for having good head knowledge about it. Mastery of total sexy health includes learning, understanding, practice, experience and wisdom. It may be helpful to have schooling and higher education, but only to some extent. Book learning and academic information miss the non-conceptual aspects of our nature. It omits experiential, physical, social and environmental realities.

Your mastery of total sexy health consists of simultaneously embodying the 8 key parts designed by nature:

- Inner awareness presence
- Life energy power
- Inspired creativity
- Fit, active and freshly fed, watered and aired
- Competent, confident and courageous survival smarts
- Comfortable personal presence in social settings
- Respect for and gratitude within nature
- Calm trust in and awareness of the infinite

By embodying these eight key parts of total sexy health, you live your life in a stable, powerful presence. People notice it, trust it and find it sexy. They look to you to lead because you know how to lead your own life. That's prerequisite to leading others into their calm and powerful presence, and embodying these same key principles.

Who are the masters of total sexy health? We don't usually think of them as sexy, but they were the 'great masters' who lived in different cultures at different times in the past, and who taught principles and methods of self-mastery to those who lived in their time and were eager to know.

Great masters both past and present are teachers of human nature. Fully present in all eight parts of their nature, and students themselves of that mastery, they coach, inspire and encourage others who want to live this kind of mastery. They're not and don't claim or pretend to be super-human. They don't come to start religions, cults and tribes. They come to teach mastery and the freedom that self-knowledge brings. They're not loud or arrogant about their mastery.

They're fully human, and practice living fully present in all of their being. The best, most dedicated and most available teachers of self-knowledge of their time, they help others to master fully present, more abundant living. In the same way as there's always a world class athlete, sculptor, musician, singer and speaker, there's always a living person who most fully embodies self-knowledge and most effectively inspires others to it.

Find such a person and learn to live in your total sexy health. They'll save you a lot of wrong turns and hard knocks on your way to self-mastery. You have limited time here, so get all the help you can. By the way, masters don't go chanting, "I'm a master. I'm a master. I'm a master." They're more likely to think of themselves as students still learning, discovering more of human nature, and excited about finding more and more of the beauty of life and being. Masters don't give themselves the title 'master'. Those who learn from them confer that title.

Modern day 'experts' have a lot of theoretical, academic and conceptual knowledge in narrowly defined areas of expertise. As facts increase, these fields become increasingly complex. As we gain more and more facts, we end up knowing more and more about less and less, as well as less and less about more and more.

Anyone can mentor you as far as they've gone. They can't teach what they don't know. Be aware of your mentors' limitations. Especially, don't blindly follow the advice of people who have not yet mastered what you want to master.

Topic

Our topic is total sexy health. It's what I'm a student of. To me, it's the most important, interesting and worthwhile mastery possible. It puts you on a foundation on which you can massively achieve whatever you set your mind to with much less effort than you'd have to make without that foundation. It makes it possible for you to write an original plan for success on your own terms. It provides you with the sexy clarity that you need to talk straight and walk straight toward your chosen goals. It connects you with the deep, quiet, confident power that takes you to your destiny.

Once you feel cared for by having become fully present

in all of your being, it's much easier to identify what you can do and what you have to give. When you embody all of your self, you're ready to be a force for good in your chosen field. As your contribution to the world, you can then direct your efforts intelligently, toward addressing the needs that harness you natural gifts, talents and abilities. What are those for you?

It may be an inspired vision you had of what could be. But it might also have to do with your own unique challenges and obstacles in life. You've survived and overcome these and now you can help others do so. You know you can help because you've done it. You're confident that others can also do it, so you model confidence for those who struggle with what you've already mastered.

It may be some injustice that you witnessed that pained you, even though you were not treated unjustly. It may be hunger that you saw, or discrimination, abuse, exploitation, poverty, war, or other kinds of suffering.

It may be an inconvenience or a hassle that you see, for which you create a solution. It may be a lack of knowledge or education that you see holds others back. Once you feel cared for, you can think globally about what it takes to live better together. Feeling cared for and whole, you recognize that all human beings can live the way you get to live. You can help others get from where they are to where they want to be.

If you were born in one of the many hells on this planet and found your way out, you can guide others on similar journeys. This is the teaching of the masters: Anyone who wants to get to mastery can do so, no matter how dark the starting point. Imagine that! What do you want to create?

What does it take? It takes living in your lit up state of being. It takes living in your total sexy health. It takes showing up like that in your world. You're meant to live present to life. And it feels incredibly good. In that state of being, you transform your world.

When you transform your habits in line with total sexy

health, you right wrongs and clean up the natural system in which your body has its existence. You inspire others to influence their grass roots connections.

What is your purpose? No one can tell you what it should be because it is your choice. A quiet or not so quiet voice within you has always yearned to live fully present and lit up from within and to be a light that lights up others. Listen to that voice. Hear it. Millions seek inspiration. You can be one who inspires them.

Something in you knows that mastery is about your nature and your possibility. In celebrating mastery, you celebrate yourself. In respecting, loving or even worshipping life, you respect, love and worship the light that you are and that every human being is. In focusing on that, you focus on the master within you.

Bring it home. Embody it. Be it. You already have it. Dig down deep. Pull it out and make it real.

What

What do you want to master? Go for it. Master it. You can. Why? You're life and human, the only two necessary conditions for success. If you were not alive, all your potential successes would be cancelled. If you weren't human, you'd not be able to dream about new possibilities. Your time would be dedicated to breathe, drink, eat, sleep, mate and relieve yourself.

My favorite dog, a smart little mini-Maltese, is so locked into physical reality and so incapable of fantasy that it doesn't know me when it sees my face and hears my voice on an iPhone FaceTime conversation. It surprises me that it won't respond to my voice or image. It recognizes me only when I'm present in person, and then it prances around and furiously wags its tail because it can't get enough of me.

Animals have sophisticated communication for the basics of physical, nature-based living, but lack the kind of thinking, dreaming and imagining that is possible for you. Of course, the gift of human mental capability comes with a curse that reminds you to use it with caution and foresight. The gift of your mind and its capacity to think and imagine is that you can create new realities that did not exist in nature. Cities, roads, paintings, air-conditioning, energy production and opera are examples.

The curse of the human mind is that you can get so involved in thinking and imagining, that you lose touch with reality and become non-functional in the physical world in which you live. This is a basis of mental illnesses. Or, you can become so locked into mental ideation that you completely disconnect from life. Irrational behaviors, outbursts, killing sprees, and justifications for what is insane, unjust and unjustifiable may result. On a group scale, people can create conflicts over different ideologies (none are real), and wars in which both sides agree to play a game in which millions of bodies are destroyed. Each side operates from unacknowledged consent to make ideology (on each side) count for more than the human beings who imagined them into being.

What's the best mastery? You already know. To me, hands down, self-knowledge or full self-presence in all of your being is the greatest mastery because it's the unshakeable, eternal, all-inclusive foundational framework on which you can build everything else in your life in the most effective way, with the least time and effort.

Find and embody core knowledge. Standing on that foundation, you feel perfectly cared for because you ARE perfectly cared for, through ups and downs, crises and disasters, situations and circumstances.

When you know that you're always cared for because you feel it, there's nothing left to do other than help care for others. Feeling cared for, you're ready to tackle the unsolved issues of your time and defeat them. Knowing you're cared for, you can include all in your efforts to improve quality of life. Feeling whole, you can focus on the issues in which you can make the biggest global contribution.

Without feeling cared for, your focus will always be on how you can get yourself cared for. You will be doing less for others because you're using everyone and every situation to get more for yourself in the hope that when you get more, you'll feel better. Sorry to blow your bubble but it doesn't work that way.

Endless Possibilities

Anything is possible. In the time we live in, people know more and more details, but can master only a minute fraction of what is known. It becomes most practical to master the most basic principles involved in living. What's most basic? You are most basic. In your life and your sphere of influence, you inform everything within and around you.

You express your state of being, for better or worse, in all you do. Your strengths show up in your home, family, business, community and all else. Likewise, your weaknesses show up in every single aspect of your life. Why?

Everything in your world is an expression, extension or expansion of your state of being, which comes from your level of self-knowledge, awareness and mastery. Like it or not, that's the truth. It's why working on your self is so fundamentally important. It's why you must first seek within yourself the state of being that you want to occupy. That's what great masters speak and live.

Every single bit of work you do on your awareness of being shows up everywhere in your life. A single insight can massively affect the quality of your life and your sexiness from the day you have that insight until the end of your body decades later. What's the power and sexiness of a thousand insights? There's much to discover about the light, grandeur and brilliance of your sexy total being. Without insights, you can easily end up weak, tawdry and tediously unsexy.

Let's assume you have done your homework on yourself, feel cared for by life, feel alive, radiant, present, fulfilled, brilliant and sexy. Now you can look at what needs to be done. Here are a few of the biggest unaddressed issues of our time.

a. **Environmental issues:**

First is the use of fossil fuels. Whatever you think about fossil fuels and climate change, you can't deny that every atom of carbon you burn takes two atoms of oxygen, which you need to breathe to live, out of your breathing air. Less dangerous, more sustainable sources of energy are available. Build them.

Second, with intelligent global water management, droughts, crop failures, dehydration, land erosion, starvation, hunger and wars over scarce resources end. Fresh water, food and land become available to all.

b. **Address global conflict and wars:**

First, all people can live life lit up from within. We can embrace the light we are, instead of ignoring it and trying to put it out in others.

Second, when we feel cared for, human beings can live in harmony, sharing instead of stealing each other's resources.

Third, all people's basic needs can be met because lit up, people share what they don't need.

c. **Address global health issues:**

First, a teachable field of health, based on nature and human nature replaces disease management that is misrepresented as health care.

Second, this knowledge is made available to citizens and institutions, worldwide.

Third, we learn and teach citizens worldwide to practice self-responsible health care.

d. **Address global education**:

First, develop a teachable field of human nature that, as a foundation, lays out ways to align with each part of nature and human nature through self-knowledge.

Second, all fields related to education incorporate knowledge of human nature into their framework and structure, including health, corrections, relationship, law/justice, work & business.

We can address the global need and benefits of self-responsible self-knowledge by means of mandatory core courses in every curriculum in grade school, high school and institutions of higher learning, globally.

14

NOW WHAT?
What's Next?

Whole

YOU FEEL WHOLE AND CARED for, filled with energy and powerfully sexy. Until you felt that way, you did only what you thought would make you feel cared for and loved. Nothing did, because the critical issue wasn't that you were NOT cared for. Your awareness was focused elsewhere, outside of you or in your thoughts. Being whole and feeling cared for was always within of you, beyond, behind or below your mind's focus.

Now that you feel whole and cared for, not everything has to be about you anymore. Feeling cared for, you can now go beyond yourself, and look, listen and feel for what needs to be done. Now, you can freely help. You want to do what needs to be done, not because it'll take care of you, but because it needs to be done, and you have empathy for life. Now, living a fulfilled life, you want to be of service. Serving is an automatic extension of feeling personally cared for and whole. How do I know? I know it from my own experience.

NOW WHAT? What's Next?

You've always been whole. There's never been anything wrong with your sexy essence, with who you really are. You've always been the light in your world, even when you were unaware of that light. Unaware of it however, you were less able to feel, think and act in line with it.

Your essence is whole in its nature, and you are whole, because wholeness is your essential nature. Celebrate that wholeness. Let it take you over and be the foundation on which you build. Make everything you build an expression of your wholeness.

There's nothing wrong with the rest of the world either. You as an individual and all of us together, fantasize problems into being. Then, we dedicate life and body to manifesting them into reality. When you express the wholeness you are, you automatically empower others to find their wholeness and give expression to it. This is what great masters of the past did, and what living masters of the present do for people living now. It's what each one of you can discover, embrace and promote.

When you prefer and commit to wholeness as your state of being, you radiate it to those in your sphere of influence. How beautiful is that, in comparison to going around looking for problems, finding something wrong with every person and situation, and complaining incessantly?

Wholeness is present everywhere and present deep within you. It goes wherever you go. It is never and can never be separate from you. Even in times of despair in your mind, wholeness remains with you because it can't separate from you. It's the most 'I AM' in each of you. That's its nature. Wholeness is your nature. When you experience darkness, it's because your awareness wandered away from the light you are.

Bring your awareness back home to that light. If you're physically sick or mentally ill, you're still whole in your essential being. If you're old, your being is not affected. It's as fresh as ever. Have you noticed that what looks out at the world through your eyes has never changed, and is the same now as it was when you were a child? You, the looker, are ageless, even as you watch your body age.

That which allows you to experience everything is your true self. Relax and let yourself go into it. Feel it. See it. Hear it. Taste wholeness. Wholeness is a sexy experience that you can have 24/7 in the eternal now.

Embody

Embody your wholeness, because it is the core of your being. Let go of the mental constructs that hold you, some of which were imposed on you and some of which you made up yourself. None of them are true. Let them go. Don't allow them to define, constrict or hold you back. And don't use them as justifications for your own corruption. You're much bigger than all your beliefs, ideals and ideas. Embody your nature. Fully embody the 8 key parts designed by nature. Remember what they are? (Include awareness, energy, inspired creative mind, body, survival smarts mind and social, environmental and universal surroundings in your being.) This is your greatness. **Greatness is sexy**.

In this, your expanded state, you embody the noblest within humanity and the greatest possible vision of reality. You see that what is real for you can be real for all. What your heart ached for, all hearts ache for. The fullness of life that fulfills you fulfills all lives. The peace that radiates from deep within you is present in all human beings.

How can you know for sure? Bring awareness in touch with peace within you and you'll know that it's always been everywhere. Peace's roots are the foundation of all creation. Peace is even deeper than biology. Embody it. Create with it a space in which others can find the embodiment of peace. Remember again and again to embody it. Live every aspect of your life aware of it. A life of peace is possible for you.

Embody a grand, global vision. Think big, because in the time you have, the thoughts you generate and the effort you make can be grand or mediocre, with no difference in cost. When you embody the infinite power of peace within you, anything's possible, and you can prove it and improve it. Embody choice, and feed the light in you, to make it grow. Starve the darkness, by taking your attention from it. What gets attention grows.

Embody presence, and make it your sexy present to the world. Embody all you are with pride and gratitude for being all you are. No part of you was made imperfect. Embody your perfection fully. Embody 'Yes' to all you are, without a doubt. Embody all the light you are without a touch of darkness. Embody that you and all people have always been awesomely sexy.

Celebrate your awesome awesomeness. Sing and dance with joy and happiness for it. Embody the magnificence of all that is. Embody the pure sexy heart you are that shines with love on everything. Embody the complete acceptance of the infinite in and as you and then enfold and accept all others into it. Embody the crown of creation and embrace the beauty of all existence. Inhale the brilliance and majesty of life in human form. Enjoy the serenade of colors, sounds, fragrances and feelings of your total sexy world.

Share

Communicate your vision. Tell everybody. Be up to something amazingly splendiferous and beautiful. Tell them what you want to do, what you will do and what you're doing now. Tell them why. Tell them your personal story. Let them know what is your drive and motive for your vision.

Here is a part of mine. On 9/11, I saw the world get entranced with the destruction that comes from discontent. As a result of the events of that day, it became clear to me that discontent people will always spread discontent. If those who know contentment don't do more for contentment than discontent people do for discontent, we don't need rocket science to know where we're headed.

Of course, that's always been true but it really hit me that day. Until then, I'd thought that my efforts toward living a life of contentment and peace were personal preferences that were my business and no one else's. On 9/11, I realized the importance of making my knowledge of this topic more public, and that's one reason why I wrote this book that you're now reading.

A few days ago, on social media, I made a comment about how it's more effective to give energy to what we want than to rail about what's wrong. Someone asked me, "Udo, how do you love someone who wants to kill you?" It's not a new question. It's a basic one we all wrestle with. If peace is what you want, give attention and energy to peace. You cannot hate your way to love. You cannot kill your way to peace. After you kill all your enemies in the name of peace, you'll still be a killer without peace.

How DO you love someone who wants to kill you? The short practical answer is: From a safe distance. But there are other answers. Cultivate, feed and grow the love within your own being. That's where it has to start. Realize it more deeply, strongly and broadly. Be the love in your sphere of influence. Be an influence in that direction in what you do.

Model loving. Babies don't slide out of mothers' wombs determined to be haters and killers. They learn from those surrounding them that it's acceptable to hate, hurt and kill. What can you learn and teach that would provide children an environment in which they learn to love and help? Is it easy? Of course, it's a challenge, but it IS possible.

Transforming people from haters to lovers is not a quick fix. You can't drop a coin in a machine and get your instant love fix. If the fix doesn't instantly materialize, you can't just kick the machine to make it happen. You begin with your own life. In your life, you have choice and control over who you become. You can access every possible state of being and insight. You can learn, and share what you know. You can't give what you don't have.

Get it. Then give it. This is as true for love, peace and health as it is for anything else. In touch with these states of being, you automatically express them in what you think, say and do. Make your commitment to what you work to manifest so strong, that no fear, hate and anger can break your connection with it.

Once you do it, you can get your friends to do it. They can get their friends to get their friends to do it. Turn it into the most exciting conversation and movement on the planet. You don't have to talk to your enemies. Some of your friends are already friends with your enemies. THEY can talk friendly with them. Before you know it, no enemy wants to kill you. Get started today.

The Biggest Splash

With one body and one lifetime, what is the biggest splash for good you can make? Do you remember as a child jumping into a puddle with great gusto, to make the biggest splash you could? Do you remember the boundless enthusiasm with which you ran and jumped, and how you formed your body into a splash-bomb? Apply that enthusiasm to create a world you're proud of.

With the same 'all-in' enthusiasm for the splash you make in life, and your talent, interest and experience, you can shake up and wake up the world. What are you passionate about and what needs to be done that's being neglected? What have you learned from your own suffering that could benefit others? Your worst nightmares and traumas can become your greatest triumphs and victories.

For me, the combination of fear, conflict and discord that characterized my war-filled childhood was so intense that it drove me, at six years old, to commit to finding a way for people to live together in harmony. It undergirded my search for answers in science, psychology and self-knowledge. My drive, interests and areas of expertise came from the hardships of those early years. Now I see those traumas as great gifts.

What is your story? What personal disaster will you transform into magnificence? What curse in your life will you turn into a blessing for yourself and others? I know that you have something like that. I know, because no parent, family or community is perfect, and no childhood lacks pain or challenge.

There's much to learn. You come into the world without a road map. You learn through trial, error, and embarrassing redirections of your innocent behavior, imposed on you by adults.

What painful memories have you not resolved because you've not yet used them as a springboard to your greater purpose? Truly, what is the biggest splash for good you can make? With what you know and the time you have, what can you do that's worth doing? What's unacceptable, and what can you replace it with and grow?

Sometimes we wrestle with conflicted feelings and emotions. Did you ever get hurt and then decide to hide the best you have from those who hurt you? It seemed safer, but it was also payback. The truth is that the only way to live without getting hurt is to live with your heart wide open. Love more, not less. Closing your heart hasn't made your life better or less painful, has it? Might as well live open, then. Hiding your heart helps no one and hurts you.

The more you practice awareness, the more powerfully you meet what comes at you without losing your peace and inner balance. Then you can make your splash for good without being sidetracked or distracted.

It helps to respond to negativity with some version of, "The fact that you're alive and human is good enough for me." Or, "I accept and respect you as a human being, but I don't give a hoot what you think about me." What other people think about you is for sure their issue. It might be your issue, too, but it's definitely theirs.

Leave their opinion and analysis with them. Don't take it on. Stay focused on making the splash for good in the short time you have. Don't try to destroy negativity. Withdraw your energy from it and let it starve. In the midst of endless distractions, keep your focus. Stay committed, and be obsessed with the sexy light you are.

Global

Think globally. If you can't expand your local project into a global one, you might have to rethink it. Many highly successful people begin their projects with global perspective, and then work their way back to local levels. That way, their project has coherent global application, with local variation. The most pressing problems have global impact. Here is my list of key projects:

a. **Intelligent global water management**: This is the single most helpful environmental issue of our time. Harness water's downhill flow in dozens of different, eco-friendly ways for energy. Enhance land fertility and food production. End droughts that lead to crop failure, dehydration, famine and refugee crises. Prevent wars over scarce resources. Key: Slow down the rate at which water that falls on land returns to the ocean. It's a simple principle but a HUGE project.

b. **Sustainable energy production**: Fossil fuels were a gift, but have become a curse. There are many other energy options. Understand the nature of the threat inherent in fossil fuels; then get serious about putting something better in place.

c. **Remedies for pollution**: Most of the poisons in our air, water, soils and foods come from the chemical and fossil fuel industries. Ending use of and dependence on them will automatically reduce pollution. Life lived without the chemicals for billions of years. And nature has a vast collection of remedies in plants, herbs and spices.

d. **Healthcare based in nature and human nature**: What you call healthcare today is not healthcare. It's disease management. It has a place, but disease management is not and should not be called health care. What's healthcare? Healthcare follows knowing and defining what health actually is. That's what we've been talking about in this book. Life invented health in nature, and everything affects health. When you give each of the eight key parts of health its due, you can live your life in total sexy health. The quality of life that health makes possible is so beautiful that it's hard to describe. Living the feeling of the state of total sexy health is profound. Then, describing it is irrelevant. Many years ago, when I asked what it was like, someone once told me, "If you don't feel it, I cannot explain it. If you feel it, I don't need to explain it." That's how it is with experience.

e. **Learning and embodying the nature of human nature**: Human beings are the central problem on this planet. What's our central problem? We live disconnected and out of touch from our own nature. The single most important global topic to address is a conversation on inner discontent, and how to live fully present in all of our nature and surroundings.

f. **Peace is already always everywhere** but only peace perceives it. That's the deepest inner foundation of our lives. We don't know peace and therefore don't live in peace. Peace is part of human nature and has roots within each one of us. To live well, give peace attention, rather than scheming how to screw up the lives of others whom, out of our own lack of awareness, we define as enemies.

g. **Education must emphasize sustainable care** for all citizens and the planet we live on. This requires the development of educational materials with the nature of human nature as their foundation.

What is your list? What projects turn you on? What sexy possibilities will you give your time and body to?

The Team

Feeling perfectly cared for by life, I'm in a position to come up with global projects, and to build my team. Who's on my team? Every human being on the planet is on my team. Why do I say that? We're all in it together. Anything anyone does anywhere affects everyone everywhere.

I can no longer sink the lifeboat I'm on because I want to teach the guy on the other end of it, whom I decided not to like, a lesson. When I sink his lifeboat, I too go down. We all live together or we all die together.

The enemy is no longer out there. The enemy was never out there, but we had room to pretend. Our creation of enemies is our enemy. Our enemy is that in us that projects enemies out there. We starve that enemy in us by focusing on wholeness, and how to make that wholeness work for all.

Every human being on this planet is on my team. For better or worse, 8 billion people are team members. We can't write anyone off because everyone affects the collective state of humanity. We all create the world from our individual state of being. Everyone affects the journey toward the global goal of living life together in harmony.

Some teammates fly highly motivated in the light direction. Others move in the same direction, but at a slower pace. Some members of the team do little to help, or don't help at all. Some on the team inhibit forward movement and actively interfere with the possibility of a world that works for all.

No matter what your story of your past is, and regardless of what's going on in your present situation, life has loved and loves you without conditions. Gratitude would be a good acknowledgement. Getting to know this unconditionally loving life would be even more powerful for you. Start now. This moment. Hold it. It is your highest purpose. It is your richest possibility. It waits to welcome you.

Acknowledgments

LET ME BEGIN BY ACKNOWLEDGING the dramas and traumas of my life. Experiencing war, hunger, flight as refugees, disconnection, violence, abandonment, rejection, horse-kicking, mean judgments, curses, bullying, drugs, pesticide poisoning, illnesses, divorce, business-destroying greed, and the rest of my experiences in the school of hard knocks motivated me to look for inner strength, self-knowledge, and solutions to the age-old issues that elude humanity's efforts to resolve them and have never been fixed.

My parents Gerhard and Senta retained dignity, even though they lived through the worst time in history. My siblings Uta, Hildrun, Arndt and Gerd saw me through my rough patches and helped me find my feet. My children Tai, Usha and Rama turned into confident, competent, responsible, caring adults in spite of me.

If it weren't for friends, compassionate strangers, life, the wise young and old ones, I would not have found my way back to the light. Among these lights in my life was my aunt Ena, who made time for me. Renee and half-assed Jack inspired a shy young man with their humility and compassion. Mr. Jones kindled my love for science. Ian McTaggert Cowan and David Suzuki catalyzed the awe I feel for living creatures, their biology, and their genetics. Alfred Adler and Rudolf Dreikurs made social responsibility and goal-oriented behavior understandable. Harold Mosak showed me what protection feels like. Linus Pauling and Albert Einstein combined science, heart, and common sense. In truth, this list is much longer, because there was a lot of light in my school of hard knocks.

In a night of sincerity based on a deep, desperate, personal need to know, a human being made of light showed up, embodying the core message of life, the master in each of us that all true masters give expression to. Here is that message, my words: '**I AM come, not to judge but to love.**'

Prem Rawat taught me how to internalize awareness to explore, discover and deepen self-knowledge. He models what being in touch with life energy looks like, sounds like, and feels like. Anthony Robbins catalyzed profoundly insightful breakthroughs and promotes my work. Deepak Chopra allowed me to talk from the heart about peace on his stage. Marshall Thurber showed me where not to go. Werner Erhard and many others put on conferences that helped sharpen my clarity on what I'm here for.

Johanna Budwig piqued my interest on the effects of fats and oils on human health. My mother Senta and my brother Gerd encouraged me to write my first book. Siegfried Gursche published that book. Rees Moerman helped me start my first of several businesses. Thomas Greither facilitated the development of some of my products, travels, and lectures to reach thousands with a message of health and its practical attainment.

Finally, there is the grandeur that infinity, nature, and life put in this package that we call human.

14 billion years and countless influences impacted what is in this book, but special thanks go to Raymond Aaron for structuring, and Cara Witvoet for shepherding me through that structure, to get it done in less than one year.

Thank you, all.

About The Author

BORN DURING THE SECOND WORLD war in Europe, Udo Erasmus sometimes says that he was born in hell and with a lot of help from visible and invisible friends, walked a long crooked path from there to heaven.

Along the way, he tried out many things and learned a lot. Every trade, every movement and every step led him to the next turn on the path to find new, different and out-of-the-box possibilities. His path includes brief jobs in several different trades: fruit picking, dairy farming, logging, mining, carpentry, house painting, clearing land, burning brush, growing food, gardening, and spraying, and he loves cutting and splitting firewood. He spent a year in medicine and several years in science research. One winter, he had a part-time job babysitting pickled fish in a fish museum. One summer, he worked for the fish and game branch. Several other summers, he worked on a drilling, blasting, and prospecting crew in the mountains of British Columbia. What all of these had in common was human interaction with nature and 'wilderness'.

He tried drugs in the 60s hippie era, couch-surfed, traded a Winchester 30-30 for a trumpet that he played on the front steps of his house after a few drinks of Southern Comfort, played flute and harmonica, sang in a choir but more often in the shower, hitchhiked for 6 days from Toronto to Vancouver without a penny to his name, camped out, started a nude beach, and lived in co-ops, communes, apartments and houses both in rural and urban settings. It was wild, but it was fun!

He got married. A lover of biology, and convinced that pregnancy is not a disease, he attended the home-births of his three children and admits that his wife did almost all the work and that his small contribution was to catch them, tie and cut their cords, and return them to their rightful owner, mom.

After being poisoned by pesticides in 1980, Udo seriously turned his passion and attention to health. He obsessively studied the literature, created a method for making good oils with health in mind, developed flax seed oil, authored several books on the effects of oils on health: *Fats and Oils*; *Fats That Heal Fats That Kill*; *Choosing the Right Fats*; *Omega 3 Cuisine*; and enthusiastically educated the public in about 40 countries on the effects of oils on health and disease.

In 1992, he developed healthy whole foods supplements for dogs, cats, and horses. In 1994, he developed an oil blend that is both better balanced and more effective than flax oil. He followed this with probiotics blends and digestive enzyme blends in 1997, and a year later developed prebiotic fiber and green blends.

He passionately gave in 5,000+ live presentations on nutrition and health, 3,000+ media interviews, 1,500 staff trainings and traveled to 30+ countries with his message on oils, health, nature, and human nature. For 15 years, he spent 6-9 months living out of a suitcase to spread the message of good oils and health.

Over the past 15 years, Udo has graced the stages of luminaries like Tony Robbins (on oils) and Deepak Chopra (on peace,) keynoted an international Brain Health conference, and lectured in conferences on five continents.

He's now writing on many different titles and topics, including an autobiography. Udo consults, presents, takes on the key global issues of our time, and spearheads several multi-trillion dollar projects on peace, health, energy, environment, and education.

Udo's fervor and fire are now focused on sustainable energy and water management, as well as healthcare based in nature and human nature, the nature of human nature, and the thirst of the heart.